The Little Mac Book

Leopard Edition

Robin Williams

Peachpit Press
Berkeley • California

The Little Mac Book, Leopard Edition

©2008 Robin Williams

Cover design and production: John Tollett
Interior design and production: Robin Williams
Back cover photo: John Tollett
Illustrations of Url Ratz: John Tollett
Index: Robin Williams
Editor: Nancy Davis
Prepress: David Van Ness

 Peachpit Press
1249 Eighth Street
Berkeley, California 94710
800.283.9444
510.524.2178
510.524.2221 fax

Find us on the World Wide Web at **www.peachpit.com**
To report errors, please send a note to errata@peachpit.com
Peachpit Press is a division of Pearson Education

ISBN-13: 978-0-321-50941-3

ISBN-10: 0-321-50941-2

10 9 8 7 6 5 4 3 2

Printed and bound in the United States of America

To my mother, Patricia Williams,
who made it possible,
and to my father, Gerald Williams,
who would have been proud.

Thank you! *Many, many thanks to Nancy Davis, John Tollett, and David Van Ness!*

Contents

The Dock

Finder Windows

Menus & Shortcuts

49

Use an Application

61

Save & Print

Close, Quit & Trash

 *Get Connected* 115

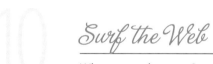 *Surf the Web* 131

Let's Do Email 147

Other Useful Features 169

Backmatter

Introduction

The Little Mac Book used to be really little—way back in 1989. In 100 pages, it told you everything you needed to know. The Mac itself was also little in those days.

Over the years, as the Mac got bigger and more powerful, *The Little Mac Book* got bigger and heavier—it finally morphed into an 850-page behemoth, and that doesn't even include information on iTunes, iPhoto, and the other cool Mac applications!

But here is a "little" book again with just the very basic information to get you started using your new Macintosh. Of course, being little means there is a lot less information! This book should get you started. When you feel the need to know more, check out *Mac OS X 10.5 Leopard: Peachpit Learning Series* for general Mac stuff, and *Cool Mac Apps, third edition* for detailed directions on how to use all the really fun stuff like iPhoto, iTunes, iMovie, iDVD, iWeb, GarageBand, and more.

Here's to a grand adventure!
Robin

A map of Your Mac

This chapter presents a very brief **overview of your Macintosh.** It provides a "map" of what you see on your monitor. In this chapter I'll give you the names of things, since it's hard to know if you need to understand more about the "Dock" if you don't know what the "Dock" is! Skim through this chapter to get the gist of what you see on your screen, then refer to the map when you need to find out where you can find specific information about a particular area.

Your Mac is full of **icons,** or small pictures. Start noticing the different icons and what you think they are telling you. For instance, icons that look like manila *folders* really are electronic "folders" in which you can store other files for organization. Icons that look like pieces of paper are *documents* that you (or someone else) created. The icon that looks like an *address book* is a small program where you can keep names and addresses. Watch for the visual clues that icons are giving you that tell you what they are and what they do.

And everything is a **file.** That is, you'll hear the term file referring to icons of every sort. It simply means any item on your computer that has a name. Your documents are files, folders are files, etc.

Mermaid Tavern

Mabel.rtf

TextEdit.app

In this chapter

The Desktop

The **Desktop** is what you see when you turn on your Mac. It's like home base; you'll get to know it well. No matter what you're doing on your Mac, you can almost always see the Desktop, at least in the background. It's just like a desk—you can spread all your work out on top of it, and no matter what you're working on, the Desktop is always underneath it all.

There will always be a menu bar across the top of your screen. See the opposite page.

This is a **Finder window.** See Chapter 4.

This icon on your Desktop represents your **hard disk,** where everything on your Mac is stored.

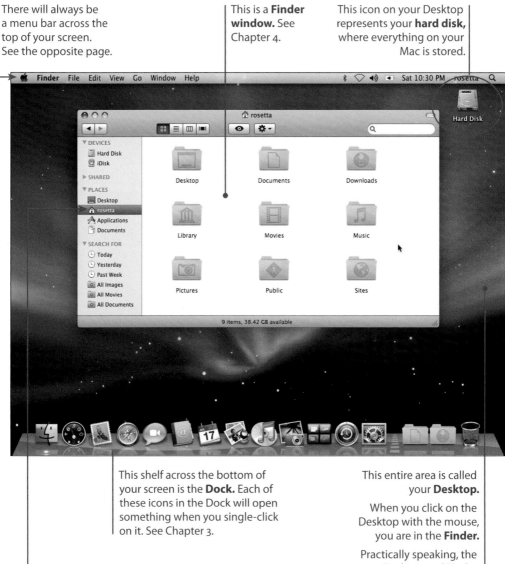

This shelf across the bottom of your screen is the **Dock.** Each of these icons in the Dock will open something when you single-click on it. See Chapter 3.

This entire area is called your **Desktop.**

When you click on the Desktop with the mouse, you are in the **Finder.**

Practically speaking, the terms Desktop and Finder are interchangeable.

This is your **Home** folder, the folder and window that you will use the most. See page 5.

As shown on the opposite page, you will always see a **menu bar** across the top of your computer screen. The items listed horizontally in the menu bar will change depending on what is "active," or front-most on your screen.

The menu bar

| ⌘ | Finder | File | Edit | View | Go | Window | Help | | 🔊 | Sat 6:16 PM | Q |

About This Mac
Software Update...
Mac OS X Software...

System Preferences...
Dock   ▶
Recent Items   ▶

Force Quit...   ⌥⌘⏏

Sleep
Restart...
Shut Down...

Log Out Robin Williams... ⇧⌘Q

This is the **Apple menu.** If someone tells you to go to the Apple menu, single-click on this Apple icon and its menu will drop down, as you see here.

Every **application** you open also has **its own menu bar,** as shown below, where you see the application called "Preview," and you see its name on the left side of the menu bar. Notice this menu bar has different items from the one shown above. Start becoming aware of the menu bar! Notice how it changes when you open different files.

Under the **Application menu,** as shown below, the last item in the list of commands is always "Quit." Also, you'll always find the "Preferences" option for every application here in its own menu.

This is called the **Application menu** because it changes to show you which application, or program, is "active" at the moment.

Tip: You might someday play a computer game or watch a DVD movie and discover that you have no menu bar. Even if the menu bar is not visible, you can always press Command Q to quit. (See Chapter 5 for details on how to use a keyboard shortcut such as Command Q.)

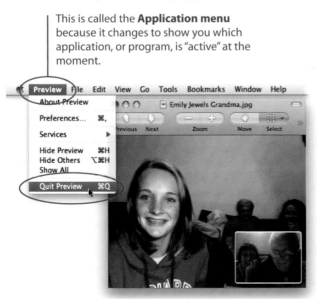

3

Finder windows

You are going to become very familiar with **Finder windows,** as shown below. Essentially the *windows* represent *folders* full of *files* (see pages 1–2 if those terms don't make sense to you).

Now, it's possible to store files all over your Desktop, but that's just like storing everything in your office right on top of your oak desk. You will get used to putting your documents into a folder and then opening the folder to view its contents in a Finder window. Chapter 4 gives you more details about windows.

Every window has a **title bar.**

The title bar tells you which **folder** you are looking at.

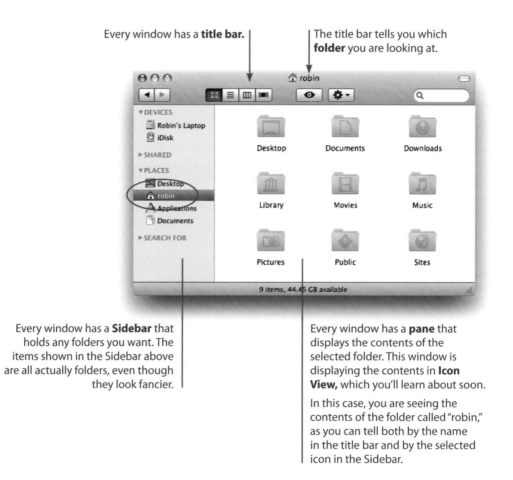

Every window has a **Sidebar** that holds any folders you want. The items shown in the Sidebar above are all actually folders, even though they look fancier.

Every window has a **pane** that displays the contents of the selected folder. This window is displaying the contents in **Icon View,** which you'll learn about soon.

In this case, you are seeing the contents of the folder called "robin," as you can tell both by the name in the title bar and by the selected icon in the Sidebar.

Apple has made it possible for a number of people to use the same computer, yet all users have their own private, protected spaces. This includes your own **Home** area, private folders, your own Desktop, your own web bookmarks and email, and your own, private Trash basket. Even if you are the only person using your Mac, you have a Home folder.

In this book I'm not going to explain how to create other users and how to take advantage of all the multiple-user features. But if you get to a point where you want to know that, it is explained in my book called *Mac OS X 10.5 Leopard: Peachpit Learning Series* (use the "Accounts" system preferences).

For now, just get used to your own Home window area and Home folders. Until you have a good reason, don't change the names of any of those folders and don't throw any of them away yet.

Desktop: This folder holds the *same* items that are on your Desktop. If you get rid of it from the Desktop, it will automatically also be removed from this folder, and vice versa.

Documents: When you save your own documents that you have created, you can always find them in this folder (unless you have chosen to store them elsewhere).

Downloads: When you copy files from the Internet onto your computer, it's called "downloading." Also, when you get photos or documents in email or on disks, transferring those files to your computer is called downloading. Everything you download will automatically go into this Downloads folder. This same folder is in the Dock, next to the Trash, so no matter what you're doing, you always have access to it.

Library: This holds hundreds of files that your Mac needs. *Do not take anything out of this folder or put anything in it!*

Movies: If you make digital movies in iMovie, your Mac will automatically store the files in this folder for you.

Music: When you use iTunes to copy music to your Mac and make your own playlists, those files are automatically stored here.

Pictures: If you use iPhoto, it will store your photos in here.

Public: This is for sharing files with other users.

Sites: This is for sharing the web sites you create. If you doubt you'll be doing that, you can throw this folder away when you do the practice exercises in Chapter 8. You can always re-create it.

Home

The folders in your Home window

Keys on your keyboard

Your **keyboard** has a number of special **keys** that you will use all the time. Some of them are called "modifier keys" because they don't do anything when you press them down all by themselves—they only make something happen when used in combination with other keys or with the mouse.

Below are the keys you will become very familiar with, if you're not already. In Chapter 5 you'll start using keyboard shortcuts to do things on your Mac, and in that chapter I'll show you the symbols for each key that you see in the menus.

These first four keys are the primary modifier keys that you'll use in shortcuts.

Shift key: This is the key, of course, that makes capital letters. It's labeled "shift."

 Command key: This is the key on both sides of the Spacebar. It usually has an apple symbol on it and it always has the freeway cloverleaf symbol. Some people call this the "Apple key."

Option key: This is next to each Command key and is labeled "option."

Control key: This is the key on the outer bottom corners of the keyboard. It's labeled "control." Be conscious of whether a direction tells you to use the *Command* key or the *Control* key!

You'll also use these other keys in shortcuts.

Spacebar: If you have ever done any typing, you know that the long bar across the bottom of the keyboard is the Spacebar and it makes the space between words. Occasionally it is also used in some keyboard shortcuts.

Caps Lock key: Push this down to type in all caps. You can still type the numbers when Caps Lock is down.

Escape key: This is in the upper-left of your keyboard, labeled "esc."

Tilde key: This is directly below the Escape key, with the Spanish tilde character on it. It looks like this: ~

Arrow keys: To the right of the main keys you might have a little set of four arrow keys. In certain programs the arrow keys will move selected items around the page.

Fkeys: These are the keys across the top of the keyboard. Many programs will let you customize what these keys do.

You might be working on your Mac and then go have a cup of tea and when you come back, **the screen is black.** Don't worry—it's okay! What happened is that the Mac noticed you weren't using it so it put itself to sleep, or at least put the screen to sleep.

To get your screen back, just tap any key at all on the keyboard or wiggle the mouse back and forth.

You can control when the computer or the screen goes to sleep. In Chapter 12 you'll read about the System Preferences, and by the time you get to that chapter you'll feel comfortable with opening the Energy Saver preferences.

When you're typing, you want to avoid using **ALL CAPS** because not only is it harder to read than lowercase, but it takes up too much space and it gives the impression you're shouting. If at some point you discover that EVERYTHING YOU TYPE IS IN ALL CAPS, you probably accidentally hit the "caps lock" key. It's on the left side of your keyboard, above the Shift key. Just tap it one more time to turn off the caps lock.

Remember

As long as you don't throw anything in the Trash just because you don't know what it is, you really can't hurt anything on your Mac.

So feel free to experiment all you want. As you work through the exercises in the following chapter, it's a good idea to start with the first one and continue on through because some of them are dependent on the previous one.

Remember that your Mac does exactly what you tell it, so it's your responsibility to learn how to tell it what you want it to do!

Have fun!

The Mouse

2

The **mouse** is one of the most basic and important tools on your computer. The combination of a mouse and icons (small pictures) is what makes the Mac so easy to use. This chapter will walk you through how to use the mouse properly, and along the way you'll learn many of the **basics** of using your Mac in general. If you're new to the Mac, don't skip this chapter even if you know how to use a mouse!

Never used a mouse before?

In case you've never used a mouse before, follow these simple guidelines:

- Keep the mouse on a flat surface, like your desk or table. That is, you don't need to point it at the screen or hold it in the air or touch it to the monitor. Just move it around on a flat, smooth surface.

- The mouse cord should be facing away from you.

- Keep one finger positioned on the end of the mouse where the cord connects. *The end of the mouse* is considered the mouse "button," even though you don't see an actual button. Now, if you have a mouse with an actual little button in the *middle*, like the one shown below-right, that is not the mouse button! Odd, isn't it? The thing that actually looks like a button is a "scroll wheel" that you can use when you get to a web page to move around the page.

  When a direction tells you to "click" on something, that's when you'll push the front end of the mouse down, the end near the cable. You will hear a "click" sound when you push in the right place.

- If your mouse has two "buttons," one on the left and one on the right, always use the left button unless I specifically tell you to use the right one. A two-button mouse almost always has the scroll wheel mentioned above.

- If you have a laptop that uses a trackpad instead of a mouse, see page 22.

- A mouse pad is a flexible little mat that helps gives your mouse traction, but it's not required. There's nothing magical about a mouse pad that makes a mouse work— you can use your mouse without any pad if you like.

If you're **left-handed,** just plug the mouse into the left side of your keyboard. You can also use the "Keyboard & Mouse" preferences to switch the primary mouse button; see page 170 about System Preferences.

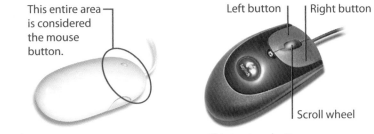

This entire area is considered the mouse button.

This is a regular mouse.

Left button | Right button

Scroll wheel

This is a two-button mouse.

Moving the mouse

As you move the mouse across the mouse pad or desk, a **pointer** moves around the screen in the same direction as the mouse.

Once you start working in different applications, the pointer will change into different shapes, sometimes generically called **cursors.** No matter what form it takes, the pointer or cursor will follow the mouse direction as you move it.

If you feel like you're having to move your mouse too far in relation to how far the pointer on the screen moves, you can adjust it: When you get to Chapter 12, read about the System Preferences and then use the "Keyboard & Mouse" preferences to make the "tracking speed" faster.

> This is the pointer you'll see on your computer screen.

- Move the mouse around and watch the pointer until you feel comfortable moving the mouse while looking at the screen.

Moving the mouse when you've run out of space

Sometimes you may be **moving the mouse** across the mouse pad or the desk and **run out of space** before the pointer or other cursor gets where you want it to go. Just do this:

1 Keep your finger on the mouse button, pressing it down.

2 Pick up the mouse, *keeping the button down,* and move the mouse over to where you have more room.

3 Then just continue on your path.

The tip of the pointer

The only part of the pointer that has any power is the **very tip,** called the **hot spot.** When you need the pointer to activate something, be sure that the extreme point of the arrow is positioned in the area you want to affect.

This is the **hot spot** . . . . .

For instance, in the exercises on the following pages you will click in the little red button of a window. Be sure to position the pointer like so:

Only the **very tip** of the pointer (the hot spot) does the trick.

Clicking the mouse

There are **four basic things** you'll do everyday with the mouse:

- Single-click
- Double-click
- Press
- Press-and-drag

On these next few pages you'll go through short exercises to understand the differences between the techniques and when to use them. It's important to go through these exercises in order because each one requires that you did the one previous!

Single-click

A **single-click** is a quick, light touch on the front end of the mouse, with the pointer (or other cursor) located at the spot of your choice on the screen. As you work on your Mac, these are the kinds of things you'll do with a single click:

- Single-click an icon on your Desktop or in a Finder window pane to *select* that icon.
- Single-click a menu to *display* its commands, as shown on page 16.
- Single-click an icon in the Sidebar of a window to *display* that item's contents in the window.
- Single-click an icon in the Dock to *open* that application or document.
- When you're typing, as described in Chapter 6, you'll single-click with an "I-beam" to set down an "insertion point" for text.

Exercise 1: Use a single-click to select an icon on the Desktop.

- If you see an icon of your hard disk in the upper-right corner of your screen, **single-click** on that icon. (If not, skip to the next exercise.)

  A single click "selects" an individual icon that is on the Desktop or inside of a window so you can do something with it. You're not going to do anything with it right now except notice it.

Note: To deselect an icon, just click anywhere else, preferably on a blank spot on your Desktop.

Robin's hard disk

This is a typical unselected icon.

When you single-click an icon, the border around it is your visual clue that it is selected.

Exercise 2: Use a single-click to open a Finder window.

- In the Dock (that bar of icons across the bottom of your screen), **single-click** on the smiley icon on the left end, which is the Finder icon.

  When you single-click an icon in the Dock, it opens that item. In this case, you have opened what's called a **Finder window.**

  If you already had a Finder window open on your screen, nothing appears to happen except that window makes itself available to you. Continue to the next exercise.

This is the Finder icon in the Dock.

This is the **Sidebar** of a Finder window.

This is a **Finder window.** Each of the folder icons inside will open to another window, as you'll learn in Chapter 4.

13

"Single-click" continued

Exercise 3: Display the contents of the Applications folder in the same Finder window.

- In the Finder window that opened in Exercise 2, **single-click** on the "Applications" name or icon in the **Sidebar.**

   When you single-click an icon in the Sidebar, that item displays its contents in the window pane to the right. These icons in the Sidebar are actually the equivalent of folders, in that they store other files for you. If your Mac is brand new, the "folders" in the Sidebar named Documents, Movies, Music, and Pictures are probably empty at the moment—that's okay. Go ahead and single-click on them to check.

Notice the name in the **title bar** of the window tells you which folder you are seeing in the window pane below.

When you single-click an icon in the Sidebar, the window pane on the right changes to display the contents of the item you clicked on. For instance, here you see the applications that are stored in my Applications folder. You will probably have different application icons in your Applications folder.

Double-click

A **double-click** is a quick click-click on the front end of the mouse, again with the pointer located at the appropriate spot on the screen. *A double-click has to be quick and the mouse must be still or the Mac will interpret it as two single clicks.* As you work on your Mac, these are the kinds of things you'll do with a double-click:

- Double-click an application or document icon to *open* that application or document (as long as the icon is not in the Dock or Sidebar—*single-click items in the Dock or Sidebar*).

- Double-click a folder icon (not in the Dock or Sidebar) to *open* the window for that folder.

- Double-click on a word to *select* that word for editing.

Exercise 1: A double-click will open icons that are *NOT* in your Dock or Sidebar.

- Double-click on the icon of your hard disk, in the upper-right corner of your screen. A double-click will "open" the hard disk and show you its window.

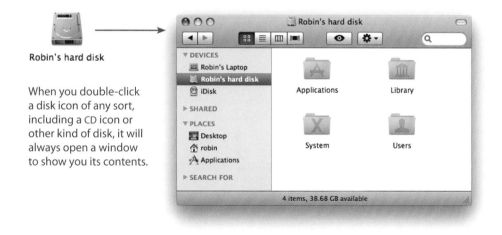

Robin's hard disk

When you double-click a disk icon of any sort, including a CD icon or other kind of disk, it will always open a window to show you its contents.

You may notice that the window for your hard disk looks different from the window you get when you click on the Finder icon in the Dock! You're right—the hard disk window shows you folders that you rarely need to use, folders that are higher up in the hierarchical structure. If you want to experiment, double-click the "Users" folder and inside of it you'll find your Home folder.

"Double-click" continued

Exercise 2: Double-click to open a folder when a window is in Icon View.

1 Your window should be open from Exercise 1 (if not, single-click on the Finder icon in the Dock to open a Finder window).

2 Make sure the window is in Icon View, as shown below. (If it isn't, click the Icon View button, which is the one on the left of the four buttons, circled below.)

3 Now double-click on a folder icon in the window pane, as shown above. It will "open" and display its contents in the pane, as shown below.

If there are no files stored in that folder, the pane will be empty. That's okay!

As explained below in Step 4, single-click this Back button to go back to the window contents you saw previously.

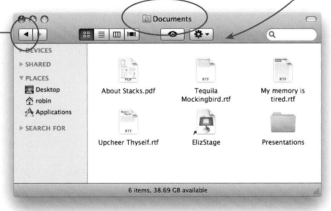

In Chapter 6, you'll double-click on a document icon (like the ones shown in this window pane) to open a document so you can work on it.

4 **To go back** to view the contents of the previous folder/window, single-click the "Back" button, circled above.

To **press** means to point to something and instead of clicking, **Press**
press the mouse button and *hold it down.*

- Press on items in the Dock to *pop up* their menus.
- Press on the arrows in a scroll bar of a window to *scroll*
  through that window.

Often directions (not mine!) will tell you to "click" on things when
they really mean "press." If clicking doesn't work, try pressing.

**Exercise 1: Open the menus that pop up from the Dock (the
shelf of icons across the bottom of your screen).**

1 **Press** (don't click!) on the Finder icon in the Dock.

  A little menu pops up; if you have more than one
  window open, this menu will list each one.

2 To make the menu go away, just drag your mouse
  off to the side and let go of the mouse button.

This is the
Finder icon.

Press on the Finder icon (don't click) and
you'll see something like this menu. The
name of each window that you have open
will appear in the menu.

Next exercise . . .

In a minute you can **scroll** through a window by pressing on the
scroll arrows. But first go to the following page and learn about
press-and-drag so you can resize your window; otherwise you
might not even see scroll arrows!

Press-and-drag

In many manuals, this technique is misleadingly called click-and-drag.

Press-and-drag means to point to the object or the area of your choice, *press*/hold the mouse button down, *keep it down,* and *drag* somewhere, then let go when you reach your goal.

- Press-and-drag to *move* icons across the screen.
- Press-and-drag to *move* a window across the screen.
- In a Dock menu, press-and-drag up the menu to *select* an item (then just let go when you select an item; don't click).
- When you're typing, press-and-drag to *select* a range of text.

Exercise 1: Move a window to a new position on your monitor.

1 If you have no window open, single-click on the Finder icon in the Dock to open a Finder window.

2 *Press* on any gray edge of the window (with the tip of the pointer, remember), *hold* the mouse button down, then *drag* your mouse. This will move the window. Wherever you let go of the mouse, that's where the window will stay.

Exercise 2: Resize a window.

1 If you have no window open, single-click on the Finder icon in the Dock to open a Finder window.

To instantly resize your window to the size it was previously, single-click the green button.

2 Locate the **resize corner** of the window, the lower-right corner that has little diagonal markings in it.

3 Press-and-drag that corner to resize the window.

This is the resize corner.

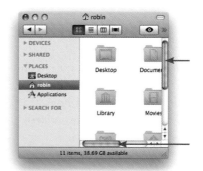

When a window is too small to display its contents, you'll see triangular scroll arrows and blue scrollers. See Exercise 3 in this section.

Exercise 3: Scroll through a window to see all the contents.

1 If you have no window open, single-click on the Finder icon in the Dock to open a Finder window.

2 Single-click on the Applications icon in the Sidebar to display the contents of the Applications folder.

3 Your Mac came with more applications than can be seen in one window pane. When you see blue scrollers or scroll arrows (shown below), it is a visual clue that there are items in this window that you can't see.

Either *press-and-drag* a blue scroller to make the contents slide by, or *press* (and hold) a black scroll arrow.

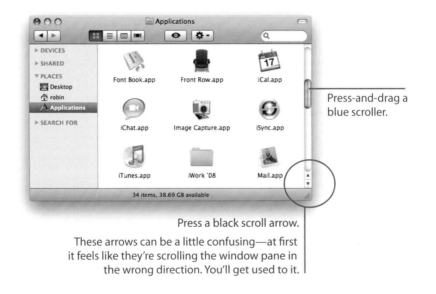

Press-and-drag a blue scroller.

Press a black scroll arrow.

These arrows can be a little confusing—at first it feels like they're scrolling the window pane in the wrong direction. You'll get used to it.

Hover

There is one more mouse technique you might want to experiment with, called **hover.** Just position the tip of the pointer over a button or icon and hold it there—*don't click, don't press, just hover.* Often a tool tip or icon name appears, as shown below. Try it!

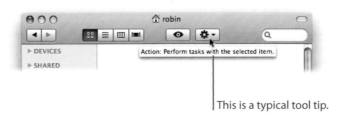

This is a typical tool tip.

Trackpads A Macintosh laptop has a built-in **trackpad** to do what a mouse does. The trackpad is a flat space on which you drag your finger to move the pointer around the screen. It takes a little time to get used to it.

- Generally, move your finger around the trackpad. When you want to click on an item, tap the bar under the trackpad (shown below).

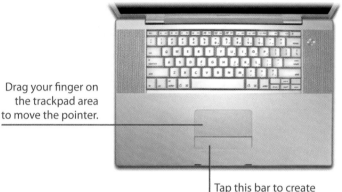

Drag your finger on the trackpad area to move the pointer.

Tap this bar to create a mouse click.

There are several controls you can set for your trackpad that can make it easier to use; when you get to Chapter 12, read about the System Preferences, then use the "Keyboard & Mouse" preferences to change the setting for the trackpad.

If you find the trackpad awkward, you can always plug a mouse into the back or side of your laptop and use that instead. Be sure to check the controls mentioned above so your Mac doesn't get confused between the trackpad and the mouse.

Also Try This

Below are a few advanced uses of the mouse. You can skip this for now and come back when you see the term and need to know how to do it.

You'll eventually see such terms as **Shift-click, Command-click, Option-click,** and **Control-click.** This means to *hold down* that key mentioned (Shift, Command, Option, or Control) and then click the mouse button once. Different things happen with each action. Try these:

- To *select* more than one icon, Shift-click individual icons (when a window is in Icon View). Shift-click also to *deselect* an item from a group of selected icons.
- Shift-click file names (when a window is in Column or List View) to *select* all of the files between the first click and the Shift-click.
- Command-click individual file names (when a window is in Column or List View) to *select* more than one file, or to *deselect* an item from a group of selected icons.
- Control-click on various items on the Desktop to get "contextual menus," which are menus that offer differ-ent choices depending on what you Control-click (see Chapter 5).
- Option-click on application icons in the Dock to give you a menu choice to force that application to quit.

You'll see directions like **Shift-drag, Option-drag,** or **Command-Option-drag,** which means *hold down* the Shift, Option, and/or Command keys and drag the mouse. Try these:

- Option-drag a file from one window to another to make a copy of that file.
- Command-Option-drag a file to another folder or to the Desktop to make an "alias" of it (alias information is in Chapter 12).

Shift-click
Command-click
Option-click
Control-click

The Shift, Option, and Control keys are all labeled on your Mac. The Command key is the one right next to the Spacebar, with the apple symbol and the cloverleaf symbol on it. See page 6.

Shift-drag
Option-drag
Command-Option-drag

23

- When using the mouse, the **tip of the pointer** is the only thing that has any power! All the rest of the pointer is dead. So make sure the very tip is touching what you want to click on.

- If you are in the process of moving the mouse and you **run out of room,** hold the mouse button down, pick up the mouse, move it over, and keep going.

- **Single-click:** Basically, single-click on any icons that are in a bar of any sort, such as a menu bar, toolbars of any kind, sidebars, the Dock, or icons in something like the System Preferences (shown in Chapter 12). Also single-click on things that look like buttons and on any tiny triangle you see.

- **Double-click:** Just about the only things you will ever double-click on are the icons on the Desktop or in a window pane.

The Dock

3

The **Dock** is that strip of icons across the bottom of your screen, and you'll find it to be one of your most important tools. In this chapter you'll experiment with using the Dock, adding icons to it and takings icons out, resizing it, and more.

If your Dock doesn't look exactly like this, don't worry—it is totally customizable!

In this chapter

All those icons in the Dock

Below is a **description of each icon** that is probably in your Dock when you first turn on a new Macintosh. Don't worry if you have slightly different icons! An asterisk (∗) under a number, shown below, means that icon will try to automatically connect to the Internet when you click on it.

Dividing line

1   2   3   4   5   6   7   8   9   10   11   12   13   14   15
    ∗   ∗   ∗   ∗   ∗

1 **Finder:** Single-click the Finder icon when you need to **open a window.** If you did the exercises in Chapter 2, you are familiar with this icon and what it shows you (if you skipped those exercises, you might want to pop back to the previous chapter and run through them).

2 **Dashboard:** Widgets provide quick information at your fingertips. See pages 183–186.

3 **Mail:** This is an **email** application that you'll use to send and receive email (unless you use America Online, in which case you don't need Mail). If by chance you have more than one email acount (for instance, one for work and one for personal mail), Mail can check them all at the same time, and it can also send email messages from any of your accounts. See Chapter 11.

4 **Safari:** This represents the software called a **browser.** It displays web pages, so this is what you'll use to surf the web (see Chapter 10). If someone tells you to "open your browser" or "open Safari," this is what you'll click on.

5 **iChat:** With iChat you can "talk" (type) to everyone else in the world who also has the type of account that lets them chat. This chatting is done "live," which means you are both at your computer at the same time and responding to each other, as opposed to an email message that waits in your box for you to open it. You can even have group chats. If you have a video camera attached, you can have free video conferences around the world!

6 **Address Book:** This is a little application in which you can collect and organize contact information such as names, addresses, phone and fax numbers, email, web addresses, birthdays, anniversaries, notes, and more. When you use the Mail program, you can get addresses from the Address Book and transfer them directly to an email message without having to type the address. See Chapter 11.

7 **iCal:** Create and manage multiple, color-coded calendars of appointments, to-do lists, and important events. Set alarms for events. Automatically send and retrieve invitations for events, and, if you have a .Mac account, you can publish your iCal calendar on the Internet.

8   **Preview:** View any photo or PDF file in Preview. This deceptively simple little application can do quite a lot—too much to explain in this book. If you find you use Preview a lot, please see the more advanced book called *Mac OS X 10.5 Leopard: Peachpit Learning Series* for details on it.

9   **iTunes:** With iTunes you can transfer songs from music CDs to your Mac so you can play them without having to have the CD inserted into the computer. You can burn CDs of your own collections; listen to radio stations over the Internet; and buy individual songs, entire CDs, and audio books right through the iTunes Music Store.

10   **Spaces:** This feature allows you to have several Desktops. You might use one Desktop for email and web surfing, another for your work projects, another for your games. See Chapter 12.

11   **Time Machine:** If you have installed a second drive into your Mac or attached one to the outside, you can use Time Machine to back up your entire computer and access any file the way it was on any particular day.

12   **System Preferences:** The Mac lets you customize many of its features. For instance, you can change the picture on your Desktop, adjust your mouse, change the time zone, and more. See pages 170–171.

Dividing line: Everything you see to the *left* of this dividing line is an icon representing an application, or program, that you use to do things with. On the *right* side, you can put your own folders, documents, web site addresses, and other things. And of course the Trash is on the right side.

13   **Documents folder:** This is a copy of the Documents folder that is in your Home folder. Because it's in the Dock and you can always get to the Dock even if you're in an application, this makes it easy to access and open any file you keep in your Documents folder.

14   **Downloads folder:** This is a copy of the Downloads folder that is in your Home folder. It stores all files you have downloaded (copied to your computer) from the web, from an email message, or from anywhere else. You can store any downloaded folder somewhere else, of course—this just makes it easy for you to find a downloaded file so you don't have to waste time figuring out where your Mac put it.

15   **Trash:** Any file you don't want anymore you can just drag to the Trash. See Chapter 8.

You might have icons in your Dock for the iLife applications: **iPhoto, iMovie, iDVD, GarageBand, iWeb.** To learn to use those, plus **iChat, iTunes,** and **iCal,** please see the book from Peachpit called **Robin Williams Cool Mac Apps, third edition,** by John Tollett (with a little help from me). It has step-by-step manuals for using these great applications—and many more.

Display item names

You can "hover" your mouse (as explained on page 21) over an icon in the Dock, and a little **tool tip** appears that tells you the name of the item.

1 Without holding the mouse button down at all, just position the mouse so the arrow points on top of an icon in the Dock.

2 *Don't press the mouse button down,* but just "hover," holding the mouse still. A tool tip appears. It disappears when you move the mouse away.

This technique is useful in many Mac applications. Try it whenever you see icons in a toolbar.

The tiny blue bubble

The tiny **blue bubble** you see under different icons in the Dock tells you that particular application is already open, even if you don't see signs of it anywhere. If you single-click an item in the Dock that has a bubble, that application will come to the front so you can work in it. The Finder and Dashboard are always open.

Resize the Dock

As you add and delete items from the Dock, the Dock gets **larger and smaller.** But perhaps you want it larger right now so you can see the individual icons better. It's easy to resize.

1 Position your mouse directly over the dividing line that is on the right side of the Dock. The pointer will turn into a double-headed arrow when you are in the right spot, as shown below.

This is what the pointer turns into when you are positioned directly over the dividing line.

2 When you have the double-headed arrow, press the mouse button down and (keeping the button down) drag the mouse slightly, up or down. As long as the mouse button is down, the Dock will resize as you drag.

If you find you never use certain applications whose icons are in your Dock, you can **remove the icons.** Don't worry—you won't destroy the original files! All you remove is a picture—you can't hurt the original application, folder, file, web site, or anything else.

You cannot remove the Finder icon or the Trash basket, though.

1 To remove an item from the Dock, press on it with the mouse button.

2 Without letting go of the mouse button, drag the icon off the top of the Dock and drop it anywhere on the Desktop. A cute little "poof" will appear.

This is the "poof" that appears when you remove something from the Dock.

To put an item back into the Dock or to put a *new* item in the Dock, see the following page.

Remove an item from the Dock

If you don't have a digital video camera yet, you might want to take iMovie out of your Dock (if it's there). Or drag the Documents folder icon out of the right side of the Dock; you can always get to the Documents folder in your Home window.

You can easily **rearrange** the items in the Dock to suit your preference. Icons must stay on the side of the dividing line they are currently on, though—you'll find it's not even possible to move something from the right side of the dividing line to the left, and vice versa.

You cannot move the positions of the Finder icon or the Trash basket.

1 Press on any icon in the Dock.

2 Without letting go of the mouse, drag the icon to the left or right as far as you want to go. You'll see all of the other icons move out of the way to make room for the one you're moving.

3 When you like the position, let go of the mouse button.

Rearrange items in the Dock

If you accidentally delete an icon, see the following page for easy directions on putting an item **into** the Dock.

Here you can see the arrow is dragging the icon to the left.

You can drag up and over the top of the Dock, but be careful not to let go when the icon is out of the Dock or you'll delete it, as shown at the top of this page!

29

Put an item in the Dock

To practice **putting an item in the Dock,** we're going to go to your Applications window and get the small word processor (an application used for typing letters or other documents) called **TextEdit.** We'll put it in the Dock so it's always available to you. You'll use this application in Chapter 6.

TextEdit.app

This is what the TextEdit icon looks like. Yours might not have ".app" at the end—that's okay.

1   Single-click on the Finder icon in the Dock to make sure you have an open Finder window.

2   In the Sidebar of the window (as shown in Chapter 2), single-click on the Applications icon. This will display, on the right side of the same window, all of the applications that came with your Mac.

3   To find the TextEdit application, type the letter **T** (this selects the first application that starts with the letter T, which is TextEdit). Or you can scroll down the window until you see TextEdit.

4   *Press* (don't click!) on the TextEdit icon and *drag* it down to the Dock; when the tip of the pointer is in the Dock, all of the other applications will move over. At that point, let go of the mouse button.

Remember, you have to put an application on the *left* side of the dividing line.

You'll notice that the TextEdit icon is still in the Applications window, *plus* it is in the Dock. That's exactly right—the Dock icon will go and get the real application that is always stored in the Applications window.

Now the TextEdit application will always be in your Dock, ready for you to use it.

You might like to make the **icons enlarge** as your mouse rolls over them. This is useful if you like to keep the Dock rather small but you want the icons to be bigger when necessary, or if you end up with so many items in your Dock that *everything* becomes very tiny. As you can see below, just the icons your mouse rolls over become temporarily bigger (the pointer below is on the iTunes icon).

Magnify the icons in the Dock

When "Magnification" is on, the Dock icons grow as you run your mouse over them.

1 With your mouse, take the pointer up to the Apple menu, the blue apple in the top-left corner of your screen.

2 Single-click on the blue apple to display the Apple menu.

3 Slide down to "Dock," then slide out to the right and single-click on the option to "Turn Magnification On." The menu will automatically disappear after you do that.

It can be a little tricky to slide out to one of these submenus. Try to go straight across, staying inside the blue line.

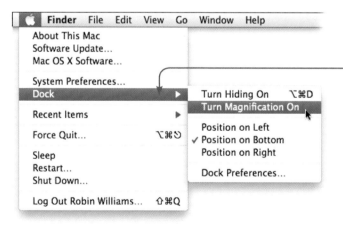

4 Now, down in the Dock, *do not click the mouse button,* but just slide the mouse over the icons in the Dock.

To turn off this feature, repeat steps 1–3 above. The option to "Turn Magnification On" has changed into "Turn Magnification Off." Choose it.

Reposition the Dock

You might like to position your Dock on the **left or right side of the screen,** instead of at the bottom. It's easy to do:

1 With your mouse, take the pointer up to the Apple menu, the blue apple in the top-left corner of your screen.

2 Single-click on the blue apple to display the Apple menu.

3 Slide down to "Dock," then slide out to the right, then down, as shown below. Single-click on the option to "Position on Left" or "Position on Right."

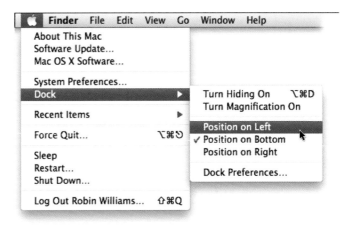

Of course, whenever you change your mind and want the Dock back at the bottom of the screen, just follow the directions above and choose "Position on Bottom."

When a Dock item jumps up and down

At some point you might see a **Dock item jumping up and down,** over and over, as if it's trying to get your attention. It is. This means that particular application needs you—click on the jumping icon and that application will "come forward." Then you will probably see a message on the screen that needs to be taken care of, such as "Do you want to save this document" or "This application couldn't do what you wanted." Just do what it wants you to do.

This is different from the "bouncing" you will see when an icon starts to open (as you'll see in Chapter 6). The bounce is little; the jump is big. It's actually kind of cute.

Here are a few more advanced features of the Dock. You don't need to know these right away, so feel free to skip this page for now.

Hide the Dock: If you find that the Dock gets in your way, you can "hide" it. When hidden, the Dock slides down under the screen; when you shove your mouse down to the bottom of the screen, the Dock automatically slides up and stays there until you choose an item (or until you move the mouse higher). **To hide the Dock,** go to the Apple menu, choose "Dock," then choose "Turn Hiding On." Of course, to turn it off so the Dock is always visible, choose "Turn Hiding Off."

Enlarge the Magnification: Go to the Apple menu, choose "Dock," then choose "Dock Preferences...." If there is no check-mark in the tiny box next to "Magnification," click in that box to check it. Then drag the little slider to the right. The farther to the right you drag the slider, the larger the icons will grow as you run your mouse over the Dock, as explained on page 31. To put the preferences away, click the red button at the top left of the window.

Force quit: If an application you're working in stops working, like the mouse is stuck or the little colored wheel is spinning forever, then you might have to **force the application to quit.** To do that:

1 Hold down the Option key and keep it held down while you do Step 2.

2 Press (don't click) on the application icon in the Dock that's giving you trouble. This makes a menu pop up.

3 The last command in the menu is "Force Quit" (because you have the Option key down; otherwise the command is "Quit").

4 Choose that command, "Force Quit." That one application should quit and the rest of your computer should be just fine. Open the application and it should be good.

Use the Dock menu: All of the commands you used from the Apple menu are also right in the Dock. To pop up the menu, hold down the Control key (not the Command key) and click directly on the dividing line in the Dock. Try it.

If your mouse or keyboard ever stops working, the first thing to do is unplug the item and plug it back in again—that almost always kicks it into working.

33

- **Single-click** icons in the Dock to open them!

- **Press** on a Dock icon to get its menu—try it.

- The tiny **triangle** underneath a Dock icon indicates that particular application is already open; single-click on it to bring it forward and work in it.

- Make the Dock work for you—reposition it, rearrange the icons, make it bigger or smaller, etc.

- If you want to know what a particular button or icon is or does, use the "hover" technique to display the tool tip, as explained on pages 21 and 28.

Finder Windows

4

A **Finder window** is a basic, fundamental element of your Mac. When you open any **folder** or **disk,** including your hard disk, the Mac displays the contents of the folder in a **Finder** window. This chapter will walk you through a number of short exercises so you'll feel comfortable using these windows.

I assume you walked through the exercises in Chapter 2 so that you know how to click, press, press-and-drag, and maybe even Option-drag!

In this chapter

The basic window

Below you see a **Finder window,** sometimes called a **Desktop window,** the kind you'll see when you open a folder or disk on the Desktop.

Later you'll work with a **document window,** the kind you'll see when you are using an application in which you create your work. The two types of windows are similar, but Finder windows have a few more features.

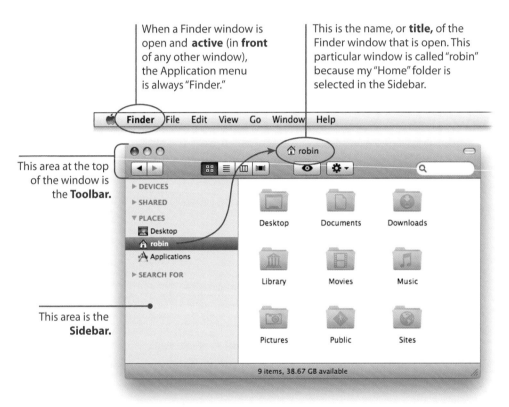

When a Finder window is open and **active** (in **front** of any other window), the Application menu is always "Finder."

This is the name, or **title,** of the Finder window that is open. This particular window is called "robin" because my "Home" folder is selected in the Sidebar.

This area at the top of the window is the **Toolbar.**

This area is the **Sidebar.**

You can tell this is a Finder window because in the menu bar across the top of the monitor, just to the right of the apple, is the word "Finder." The Finder is the software that runs the Desktop, so all of the windows on the Desktop are considered Finder windows. Don't let that confuse you—just think of the Desktop and the Finder as the same thing, for all practical purposes.

The items inside a Finder window might be shown as icons, as a list, or in columns, as explained on the following pages.

You can change how you **view the contents** of a Finder window. Some people like to see their window's contents as icons in **Icon View;** some prefer a list of names in **List View;** others prefer columns showing the contents of multiple folders at once in **Column View;** and some like the graphic **Cover Flow View.** In the short exercises that follow, you'll experiment with viewing the windows in different views.

Four window views of the same contents

These are the View buttons you see in the Toolbar — click one to change the view of the "active" window (the window in front of all others).

Below you see a Finder window in **Icon View.** Each icon represents a file of some sort. It might be a document, a folder, an application, a disk, or something else.

Icon View

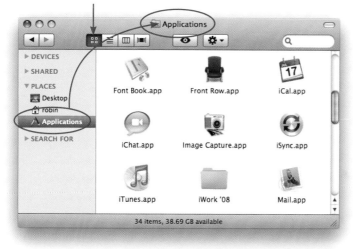

Exercise 1: Experiment with views and with Icon View.

1 If you don't have a Finder window open, do this: In the Dock, single-click the "Finder" icon (shown to the right).

2 In the Sidebar of the window, single-click the "Applications" icon. The contents of the Applications folder appears in the window pane.

3 Now click the View buttons one at a time to see how the contents appear in each of the different views.

4 Go back to the Icon View: single-click the far-left View button.

5 When in Icon View, double-click any **folder** icon to see the contents of that folder (the new contents will replace what you currently see in this window).

6 Single-click again on the Applications icon in the Sidebar to view the Applications window again.

Finder icon:
Single-click this to open a Finder window.

If you accidentally double-click on an icon that is **not** a folder, it will **open** that application. **To quit,** click once on the menu to the right of the blue apple, slide your mouse down to the bottom, and click once on "Quit."

List View   Below you see a Finder window in **List View.** Notice there are little triangles to the left of each folder icon. You can single-click on any number of triangles to display the contents of folders. This way you can see the contents of more than one folder at a time.

Single-click on the triangle pointing to a folder to display a sub-list of what is contained in that folder.

Or double-click a folder icon to display its contents in this window.

Exercise 2: Experiment with List View.

1   Click the center of the three View buttons.

2   When in List View, single-click any "disclosure" triangle next to a folder to display its contents in a sub-list in this same window.

You can open more than one folder in this way; try it.

3   **To see the contents of just that folder,** double-click any folder icon; the contents of the folder you double-click will *replace* the contents you see at the moment.

4   **To go back** to the previous window pane of contents, single-click the Back button, the triangle in the upper-left corner of the Toolbar.

Exercise 3: Resize the columns in List View to suit yourself.

**Resize the columns
in List View**

1 Using the mouse, position the pointer directly on the
dividing line between columns of information. When
you are positioned correctly, the pointer changes into
a two-headed arrow, as shown circled below.

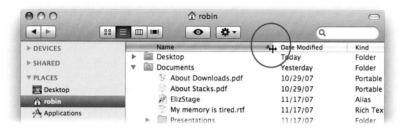

2 When you see the two-headed arrow, press-and-drag left
or right to resize the column. The column to the *left* of
the two-headed arrow is the one that will be resized.

**Exercise 4: You can rearrange the columns in List View to suit
yourself.**

**Rearrange
the columns
in List View**

1 Using the mouse, position the pointer directly on the title
of the column that you want to move.

2 *Press* the mouse button down and start to drag towards
the left or right—as soon as you start dragging, the
pointer turns into a grabber hand, as shown below.

3 Continue dragging to the left or right. When you have
dragged far enough, the other columns will shift over
to make space for the one you are moving.

4 Just let go of the mouse button when the column is
positioned where you want. (You can't move the Name
column.)

Column View   Below you see a Finder window in **Column View.** Notice there are little triangles to the *right* of each folder icon. The triangles indicate the contents of those folders will appear in the column to the right if you single-click on the folder name.

The name in the **title bar** is the name of the **selected folder** (not the name of the document that may be selected within that folder).

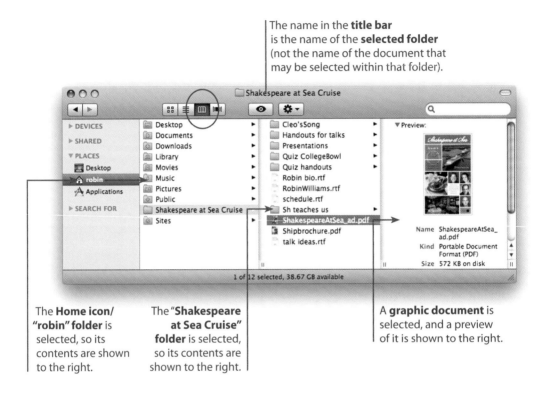

The **Home icon/ "robin" folder** is selected, so its contents are shown to the right.

The "**Shakespeare at Sea Cruise" folder** is selected, so its contents are shown to the right.

A **graphic document** is selected, and a preview of it is shown to the right.

Exercise 5: Experiment with Column View.

1 Single-click the Applications icon in the Sidebar. (You can single-click your Documents icon, if you like, as shown above, but you might not have anything in that folder yet.)

2 Single-click the Column View icon in the Toolbar, as circled above.

3 In the first column of files, single-click any folder icon to see its contents displayed in the next column.

If you see another folder to the right, single-click that one to display its contents in yet another column.

Your Mac will keep making columns to the right until you select a *document* of any type (as opposed to a *folder*). When you select a document, a small preview of some kind will be displayed in the last column.

You can **resize the columns** in Column View. You may have noticed the little "thumbs" at the bottoms of the column dividers (circled below).

Resize the columns in Column View

This is a column **thumb.**

Drag a thumb to resize **one** column.
Option-drag to resize **all** columns.

Exercise 6: Resize the columns in Column View.

1 **To resize one individual column at a time,** just press-and-drag left or right on any thumb. This will resize the column to the *left* of the selected thumb.

2 **To resize all columns at once,** hold down the Option key while you drag the thumb left or right. This makes *all* columns proportionally larger or smaller as you drag.

These two exercises are just reminders that you learned how to **resize a window** and how to **scroll through** one in Chapter 2.

Resize any window

Exercise: Resize a window.

1 Find the bottom-right corner of the window, the one with the little hatch marks in it.

2 Press-and-drag that corner to **resize** the window.

Exercise: Scroll through a window.

Scroll through any window

1 In any window in any view, **press** on any blue scroller **and drag** it up or down (or left or right, if horizontal). The contents of the window will scroll past.

2 Or **press** on one of the four tiny triangles in the bottom-right corner of a window. This will also make the contents of the window scroll past.

Cover Flow View

Below you see a Finder window in **Cover Flow View.** This is quite different from the other views in that it shows you a graphic image of each item in a folder.

- To skim through the images, either "press-and-toss" the files on either side of the center image to flip through them (try it!), **or** drag the slider in the bar beneath the images, **or** press on the arrow at either end of the bar.

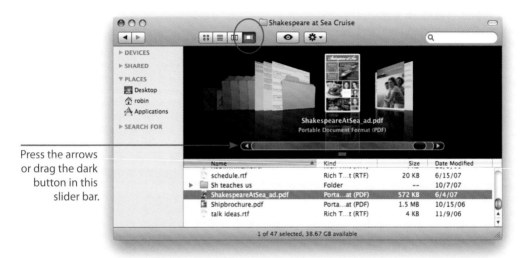

Press the arrows or drag the dark button in this slider bar.

Quick Look/ Slideshow

The button in the toolbar with an eyeball on it is the **Quick Look/ Slideshow** button. This shows you an instant preview of any file, photograph, graphic image, document, or whatever, without opening any application.

If the file has more than one page to it, or if you select more than one item, you'll have slideshow buttons to go back and forth between the images.

Exercise: Experiment with Quick Look/Slideshow.

1 Single-click on an icon.

2 Single-click the Quick Look button.

3 To view another file, single-click on it.

4 To put the Quick Look away, hit the Spacebar or click the **X** in the upper-left corner of the Quick Look window.

The Sidebar

You have used the **Sidebar** a number of times already. Here are a couple of extra tips, as well as a press-and-drag practice.

Add items to the Sidebar

You can **add other items to the Sidebar.** You might want to add files or folders that you use the most often. You might want to put a current project folder here, or, if your Dock is getting over-crowded, a favorite application.

Exercise: Add an item to the Sidebar.

1 Find the item that you want to add to your Sidebar.

2 Drag that item's icon to the *bottom* half of the Sidebar, below the horizontal dividing line.

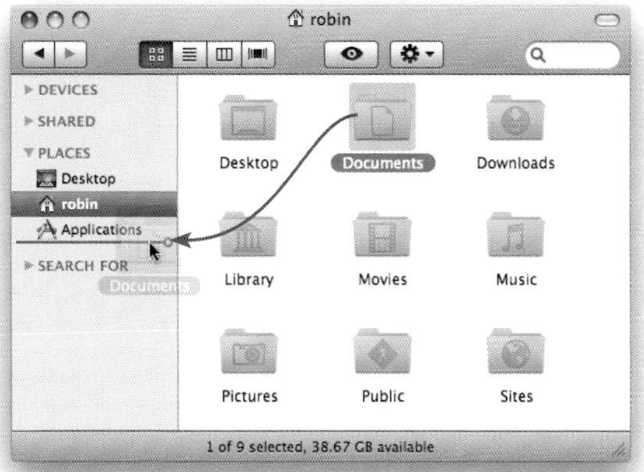

As you drag an item to the Sidebar, a blue, horizontal line appears. This line indicates where the item will be placed when you let go. If this isn't where you want it to be placed, drag up or down in the list until the horizontal line is in the position you want.

Remove items from the Sidebar

You can **remove any item** from the Sidebar. This doesn't destroy anything! You are only removing an icon that *represents* the original file—you are not deleting any original files at all.

- To remove any item from the Sidebar, just drag it to the Desktop and it disappears in a puff of smoke, as shown below.

Drag an item out of the Sidebar to remove it.

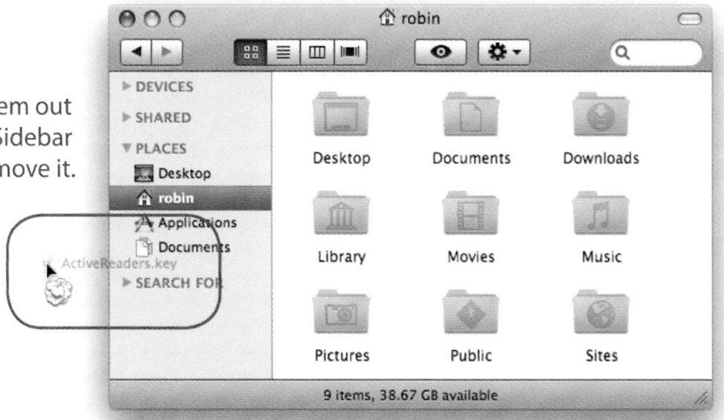

43

Window buttons   In the upper-left corner of each window are **three little buttons: red, yellow,** and **green.** These are in color in the *active* window (the one in front) and gray in all other windows behind that one.

From left to right, the buttons are red, yellow, and green.

When the pointer is positioned near the buttons, tiny symbols appear inside the buttons.

Close a window (red button)   Use the **red button,** the Close button, to **close a window.**

1 If you don't have a window open, single-click on the Finder icon in the Dock to open one.

2 To close the window, single-click in the red button. This puts it away, back into the folder or disk it came from.

Zoom a window (green button)   Use the **green button,** called the Zoom button, to zoom a window **larger or smaller.** How large or small the window becomes depends on what is in the window and how large or small it was before you clicked the button.

1 If you don't have a window open, single-click on the Finder icon in the Dock to open one.

2 Single-click the green button to zoom the window large enough to see everything, or to zoom it smaller.

When you **minimize a window,** you send a tiny icon of that window down to the Dock, on the *right* side of the dividing line. Whenever you want to see that particular window again, you can open it straight from the Dock.

Exercise 1: Minimize the window.

- Single-click the **yellow** button to **minimize** the window, which sends the window down into the Dock, as shown below.

   Or double-click in the title bar.

This is the minimize button.

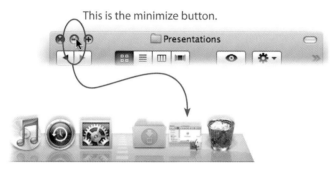

When a window is minimized, it floats down into the Dock as an icon, out of the way until you need it again. When you want it back, simply single-click on its icon.

Exercise 2: Open a minimized window.

- To open a minimized window, single-click on its icon in the Dock.

Useless-But-Fun Tip:
To minimize an open window in slow motion, hold down the Shift key when you click on the yellow button or when you click on a window icon in the Dock.

**Enlarge the icons
or the text**

You can **customize** many things about the windows. Each view has its own options for customizing. When you're ready, check these out.

To change a window's **View Options,** click on a Finder window, then go to the "View" menu and choose "Show View Options."

If the selected window is in Icon View, the pane shown on the left opens. *The options shown in this pane change when the selected window is in List View or Column View;* check them out.

Close button.

The title bar (circled above) displays the name of the **selected window.**

- Drag the **Icon size** slider to make icons larger or smaller.

- Resize the text names under icons with the **Text size** pop-up menu: Single-click the bar (the one that now says "12 pt"), then single-click on a larger or smaller number.

- Choose a **Label position** of "Right" to make icon labels (names) display to the right of icons instead of centered below them.

Upcheer Thyself.rtf   My memory is tired.rtf   Presentations 5 items

These icons have their labels on the right
instead of at the bottom.

- The changes you make will affect only the open window. If you want the changes to apply to all windows in this view, click the button at the bottom to **"Use as Defaults."**

- **To put the View Options away,** single-click the tiny round button in the upper-left corner, on the title bar.

There are two items in the "View" menu that pertain only to windows in Icon View: **Clean Up** and **Arrange.** If your window is in any other view, these items are gray, which is a **visual clue** that you can't use them.

There is an invisible underlying grid in every window, and when you choose to **Clean Up** the window, the Mac moves each icon into the nearest little square on that grid, the nearest square that the icon is already next to. This means there might still be gaps between icons, depending on where they were originally.

When you choose **Arrange** plus one of the options from its sub-menu, the Mac moves each icon into that particular order. The icons are placed in neat rows and fill every invisible square in order.

Clean up the arrangement of the icons

Exercise: Clean up the icons.

1 Open a window and view it in Icon View.

2 Using the mouse, drag the icons around in the window so they are a mess.

3 From the "View" menu, choose "Clean Up" and see what happens.

4 Now from the "View" menu, choose "Arrange By" and "Name" and see what happens.

If you don't know how to use menus yet, read Chapter 5, then come back here to experiment.

If the icons won't move into new positions, check the View Options (as described on the previous page) and make sure the menu option for "Arrange by" is "None."

View	
✓ as Icons	⌘1
as List	⌘2
as Columns	⌘3
as Cover Flow	⌘4
Clean Up	
Arrange By ▶	
Show Path Bar	
Hide Status Bar	
Hide Toolbar	⌥⌘T
Customize Toolbar...	
Show View Options	⌘J

Name	^⌘1
Date Modified	^⌘2
Date Created	^⌘3
Size	^⌘4
Kind	^⌘5
Label	^⌘6

- You will eventually figure out which **view** you like best for your windows. You might discover that you like some windows best in a list and some as icons, and sometimes you'll want to switch into Column View or Cover Flow View.

- Everything in a Finder window uses a **single click,** *except* when you want to *open* a folder icon into the window pane.

Menus & Shortcuts

5

Wherever you are on your Macintosh, you'll see a **menu bar** across the top of the screen, as shown below. Also shown below is a **menu:** When you single-click on a word in the menu bar, a list of menu commands drops down. This chapter discusses various sorts of menus, the commands, and how to use them.

In this chapter

Choosing a menu command

There are two ways to **choose a command** from a menu. Both are explained below, and you can usually use either method.

The method used in Exercise 1 is basically single-click, slide the mouse, then single-click.

The method you'll practice in Exercise 2 is press-and-drag, then let go.

Single-click, slide, single-click

Exercise 1: Display and put away menus.

1 Single-click on any of the choices along the menu bar at the top of the screen. The menu will pop open for you.

2 As you did in Chapter 2, slide your mouse (don't *press* the mouse button down!) along the menu bar horizontally and you will see each menu drop down.

3 On one of the menus, slide your mouse down the list of commands (don't *press* the mouse button down). As the pointer passes over the different choices, each one *highlights,* or becomes selected.

4 **To put the menu away** *without* selecting a command, slide your mouse off to the side and single-click on a blank area of the Desktop.

Exercise 2: Choose a menu command.

If there is no Finder window open, single-click the Finder icon in the Dock.

1 Single-click any blank spot in the window to select that window.

2 **Single-click** on the "View" menu name in the menu bar.

3 There is a checkmark next to one of the first four items in the View menu, indicating the chosen view for that particular window. **Slide** your pointer down the menu and **single-click** on a different view.

Notice the menu disappears as soon as you click, and the view of the window has changed.

Choose another view for your window.

The other method of choosing a menu command, the press-and-drag method, can be used on any menu anywhere on the Mac. Remember, **press** means to hold the mouse button down and keep it down—don't click!

Press, drag, let go

Exercise 3: Use a press-and-drag to select a command.

1 If there is no Finder window open, open one now (single-click the Finder icon in the Dock).

2 **Press** on the "View" menu in the menu bar; keep the mouse button down.

3 **Drag** your pointer down the menu and **let go** (don't click!) on a different view.

There is one time in particular when you *must* use this method, and that's when **choosing a menu item in the Dock.** As you know, if you single-click an item in the Dock, that item opens. So you must *press* on the item instead and wait a second for the menu to pop up, as described in the exercise below.

Exercise 4: Open a Dock menu.

1 **Press** on any icon in the Dock; *keep the mouse button down.*

2 A Dock menu pops up. You don't need to choose anything right now—this is just an exercise so you'll know how to do it when necessary.

3 To put a Dock menu away, just **drag** your mouse off of the menu and **let go.**

What you see in a Dock pop-up menu depends on the item and what you have been working on. For instance, if you have several Finder windows open, they will all be listed in this menu.

Gray vs. black commands

In a list of menu commands, some **commands** are in **black** letters and some commands are in **gray.** When a command is gray, it means that particular command is not available at that moment.

The most common reason a command is unavailable is because you did not *select* something *before* you went to the menu. For instance, you cannot choose "Open" from the File menu until you *select* a folder or file as the item to be opened. You cannot "Duplicate" a file unless you first *select* the file you want to duplicate.

An important rule on the Mac is this: **Select first, then do it.** Typically you select something by single-clicking on it.

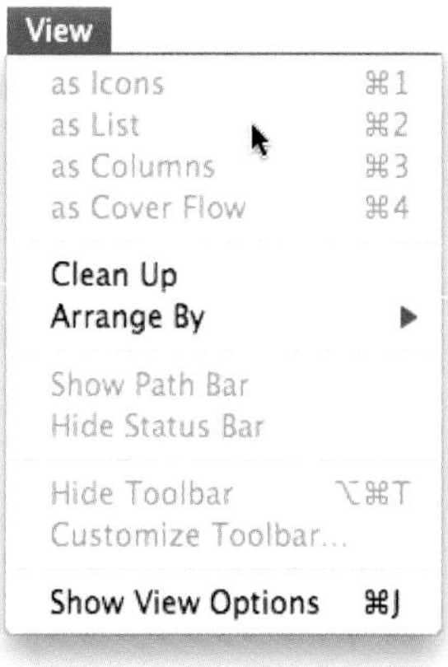

View	
as Icons	⌘1
as List	⌘2
as Columns	⌘3
as Cover Flow	⌘4
Clean Up	
Arrange By	▶
Show Path Bar	
Hide Status Bar	
Hide Toolbar	⌥⌘T
Customize Toolbar...	
Show View Options	⌘J

View	
✓ as Icons	⌘1
as List	⌘2
as Columns	⌘3
as Cover Flow	⌘4
Clean Up Selection	
Arrange By	▶
Show Path Bar	
Hide Status Bar	
Hide Toolbar	⌥⌘T
Customize Toolbar...	
Show View Options	⌘J

Some commands are gray; some are black. In this example, the different views are gray because no window is selected. If no window is selected, the Mac has no idea what to do with those commands.

This is the same menu as shown to the left, but this time I selected a window. Now I am able to change the view of the selected window.

Exercise 1a: Check the commands in the View menu.

1 Single-click on a blank area on the Desktop so nothing is selected, not even a folder or window.

2 Single-click on the "View" menu and notice how many items are gray and thus unavailable.

Exercise 1b:

1 If a Finder window is not open, open one now (single-click on the Finder icon in the Dock).

2 Single-click anywhere on a Finder window to *select* it.

3 Single-click on the "View" menu and notice how many items are now black and available.

In some programs the menu itself contains a pop-out menu where you not only slide down, but also out to the side, usually in the direction of the arrow. These are known as **hierarchical menus,** or **h-menus.**

Hierarchical menus

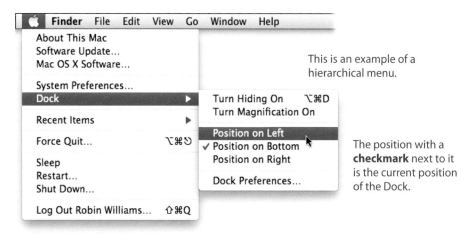

This is an example of a hierarchical menu.

The position with a **checkmark** next to it is the current position of the Dock.

Exercise: Use a hierarchical menu.

1 Single-click on the Apple menu, as shown above.

2 Slide down to "Dock." Notice it has an arrow to its right, indicating it has a hierarchical menu.

3 Slide your mouse right *across* the blue line (it can be tricky!) until you get to the h-menu, then slide *down*.

4 Single-click on a different position for your Dock.

To put your Dock back where you want, repeat the steps above and choose the position you like best.

Ellipses in the menus

Often you will see an **ellipsis** (the three dots **...**) after a menu command such as "Open**...**" or "Save As**...**." The ellipsis indicates that you will get a **dialog box** when you choose that command. *If there is no ellipsis, that command will activate as soon as you select it.*

There are different varieties of dialog boxes, such as alert boxes, message boxes, and edit boxes, plus dialog "sheets" that drop down from the title bar, but basically they all are meant to communicate with you before they activate a command.

A good dialog box will usually give you a **Cancel** button to make sure that anything you touched will not actually go into effect. If there is no Cancel button, click the **red close button** in the upper-left of the window or the blue "Done" button.

View	
✓ as Icons	⌘1
as List	⌘2
as Columns	⌘3
as Cover Flow	⌘4
Clean Up Selection	
Arrange By	▶
Show Path Bar	
Hide Status Bar	
Hide Toolbar	⌥⌘T
Customize Toolbar...	
Show View Options	⌘J

This menu command has an ellipsis, which means something will appear when you choose it.

Exercise: Experiment with ellipses in menus.

1 Open a Finder window, if one isn't already open (single-click on the Finder icon in the Dock). Single-click anywhere on the window to make sure it is *active,* or *selected.*

2 Single-click on the "View" menu.

3 Notice the command "Customize Toolbar..." has an ellipsis. Single-click on this command.

4 From the selected window, a "sheet" will drop down out of the title bar. Pretty cute, huh. You can play around with the options in this sheet.

5 When you're finished, single-click the blue "Done" button.

All over your Mac you'll find what are called **contextual menus,** menus that vary depending on what you click upon. You'll find different contextual menus in different icons, on a blank spot inside a window, a blank spot on the Desktop, in different applications, etc.

Contextual menus

To get a contextual menu, hold down the Control key (the key in the far-left or far-right corner of the main part of the keyboard), then click on anything and see what pops up.

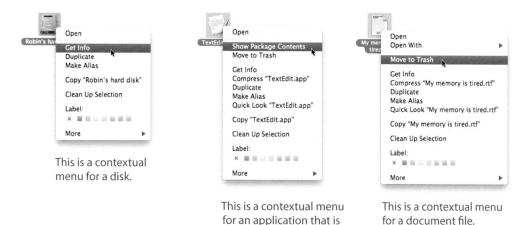

This is a contextual menu for a disk.

This is a contextual menu for an application that is "packaged" into one icon.

This is a contextual menu for a document file.

Exercise: Use contextual menus.

1 Hold down the **Control key** and click on a folder, *or* on a blank spot in a window, a disk icon, a document, *or* an application.

2 For now, just take a look at the options in the different contextual menus.

3 **To put away a contextual menu,** let go of the Control key and click on an empty spot on the Desktop or window.

If you have a **two-button mouse,** you can use the right-hand button to open contextual menus *without* holding down the Control key! Try it.

Two-button mouse

55

Keyboard shortcuts

To the right of the commands in the menus you often see a little code, such as ⌘N (pronounced "Command N"). This is a **keyboard shortcut** you can use *instead* of using the menu. You memorize the shortcut, then the next time you need that command you use the shortcut *instead* of picking up your mouse and pulling down the menu.

File	
New Finder Window	⌘N
New Folder	⇧⌘N
New Smart Folder	⌥⌘N
New Burn Folder	
Open	⌘O
Open With	▶
Print	
Close Window	⌘W
Get Info	⌘I
Duplicate	⌘D
Make Alias	⌘L
Quick Look "Morn.rtf"	⌘Y
Show Original	⌘R
Add to Sidebar	⌘T
Move to Trash	⌘⌫
Eject	⌘E
Burn "Morn.rtf" to Disc...	
Find...	⌘F
Label:	
× ▪ ▪ ▪ ▪ ▪ ▪ ▪	

Often a keyboard shortcut includes other symbols representing other keys, as described below.

Modifier keys and their symbols

A **modifier key** is a key that doesn't do anything when you press it all by itself. For instance, when you press Shift, nothing happens; when you press the Command key, nothing happens. A modifier key makes other keys perform special functions. For instance, when you hold down the Shift key and type the number "8," you get an asterisk (*).

These are the **symbols** that represent the keys you will see in the menus for shortcuts.

⌘ Command key   ⇧ Shift key

⌃ ⌃ Control key   ⌥ Option key

⎋ Escape key   F1–F15 Fkeys

⇢ ⇠ ↑ ↓ Arrow keys   ⌫ Delete key

⇞ PageUp key   ⇟ PageDown key

To use a keyboard shortcut instead of the menu command, hold down the **modifier key** or **keys** you saw in the menu. While you hold down this key or keys, type the **letter key** you also saw in the menu—*just tap the letter, don't hold it down!* The computer reacts just as if you had chosen that command from the menu.

How to use
a keyboard shortcut

For instance, if you single-click on a file to select it and then press ⌘O, the selected file will open just as if you had chosen that command from the File menu with the mouse. Thoughtfully, many of the keyboard shortcuts are alliterative: ⌘**O o**pens files; ⌘**P p**rints; ⌘**D d**uplicates a selected file; ⌘**W** closes **w**indows; etc.

You'll often see keyboard shortcuts spelled out with a hyphen, a plus sign, or perhaps a comma between the keys. **Don't type** the hyphen, plus sign, or comma! Just press the keys!

For instance, if you see a shortcut written as:

    Command + Shift + B

ignore the plus signs—just *hold down* the Command and Shift keys, then *tap* the letter B.

Exercise 1: **Use a keyboard shortcut.**

1 Single-click on the "File" menu in the Finder. Notice that Command N is the shortcut to create a **n**ew Finder window, and Command W closes a **w**indow.

Single-click on the Desktop to put the File menu away.

2 If there is no Finder window open on your Desktop, single-click the Finder icon in the Dock.

If there is a Finder window open, single-click on it to select it (remember, keyboard shortcuts only work on selected items).

3 Hold down the Command key and tap the letter W once. The selected window will close.

Exercise 2: **Use more keyboard shortcuts.**

1 You already learned that to make a new Finder window, the keyboard shortcut is Command N (N for New, of course). So simply hold down the Command key and tap the letter N once.

2 To make more Finder windows, hold down the Command key and tap the letter N several times in a row.

3 **To close all open windows,** use Command Option W: hold down both the Command *and* Option keys, then tap the letter W just once.

Other menus   You'll find other menus in all kinds of odd places. Well, they won't seem so odd once you become accustomed to the **visual clues** that indicate a menu is hiding. In the dialog box below, can you see the menus?

Double arrows   **Double arrows** are one visual clue that a dialog box contains a menu. Whenever you see that double arrow, as shown below, you can click anywhere in that horizontal bar and a menu will pop up or down.

Do you see the three menus in this dialog box? You recognize them by the double arrows.

Single arrows or triangles on buttons   A **single** downward-pointing **arrow** or a **blue triangle** in a button all by itself *is not* a menu! This is called a disclosure triangle and typically expands a dialog box to present more information, as shown opposite. The fact that this information is hidden indicates that it is not necessarily critical at all times—you only pop open that information when you need it. As you are learning to use your Mac, click that arrow or triangle whenever you see it so you become familiar with the options, whether you use them or not.

Below is a typical dialog box in which you save your new document with a name. The **default** (the automatic choice) is to save your document in the folder called "Documents." This is perfectly fine. But if you'd rather save the file into a ***different*** folder, click the downward triangle and find the folder of your choice, as shown to the right.

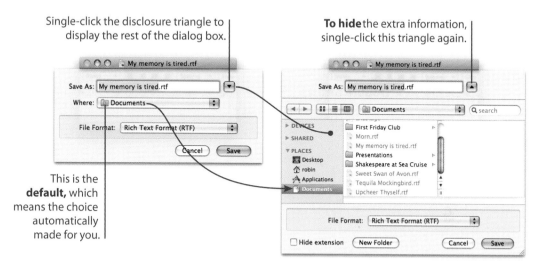

Single-click the disclosure triangle to display the rest of the dialog box.

To hide the extra information, single-click this triangle again.

This is the **default,** which means the choice automatically made for you.

You will regularly see little **color wells** (shown circled, below) in places where you can choose to change the colors of things. Whenever you see one, simply single-click on it to make the "Colors" palette appear.

Color wells

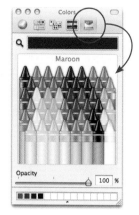

This is the View Options for a Finder window. You can change the background color of the window.

In the application called Keynote, click on the color well to change the color of **selected** text.

When you click on a color well, this Colors palette appears. Above, the crayon box icon in the toolbar is chosen. You can choose another icon in the toolbar for different options for choosing colors.

59

Remember

- Before you choose something from a menu, make sure you **select the item** to which you want the command to apply.

  For instance, if you want to close a window, first single-click on the window you want to close. If you want to make a duplicate of something, first single-click on the item you want to duplicate.

- Take advantage of the **keyboard shortcuts.** Check the menu to first find out what the shortcut is, then later use that shortcut *instead* of going to the menu.

- Did you notice in the contextual menus on page 55 that there is an option called **Label** with colored dots? You can choose one of those colors and it will make the selected icon that color. This can be a handy organizing tool—color all your love letters red, all tax files mustard, all research papers blue, etc. Later, you can search for files of a particular color of label (see pages 174–177 about searching).

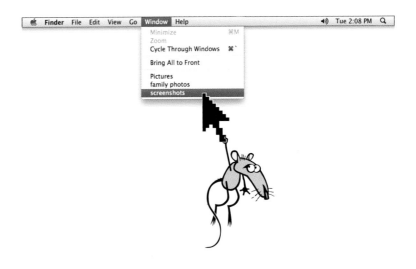

Use an Application 6

This chapter covers what you will do most often on your Mac: **open an application** and **type a document.** In the following chapter, you'll save the document, print it, close it, and quit the application.

You're going to use the TextEdit application in this chapter, but the process will apply to any application you ever use: First, you have to open the application. Then you open a document within that application. You do some sort of work on it. Most of the time you will print it, you'll always save it, then quit. So don't go through the exercises in these two chapters as if you are learning how to use TextEdit—you are learning the process of creating new documents on your Macintosh.

Almost everything you learn in this chapter will also apply to writing email, so be sure not to skip this!

In this chapter

Open an application

An **application** is a program in which you do things, like write letters, design flyers or artwork, organize and edit your photos, make movies, send email, etc. Different applications have different purposes. In this chapter you're going to open and work in a **word processor,** which is a program specifically meant for typing. Other applications are for creating databases or spreadsheets, or for painting, drawing, or building web pages, etc. In Chapter 10 you'll use an application called a **browser** that is specifically for viewing web pages.

The word processor you'll use in this chapter is called TextEdit and it came with your Mac. If you did the exercises in Chapter 2, TextEdit is now in your Dock; if not, you'll put it there in Exercise 1b, below.

TextEdit.app

Exercise 1a: Open TextEdit if its icon is in your Dock. (If not, skip to Exercise 1b.)

1 Locate the TextEdit icon in your Dock.

2 Single-click on the icon.

OR . . .

Exercise 1b: Open TextEdit if its icon is NOT in your Dock.

1 Here is a **keyboard shortcut** (you learned how to do keyboard shortcuts in Chapter 5) to open your Applications folder, whether or not there is already a Finder window open:

Command Shift A

Which means you hold down *both* the Command and Shift keys, and while they are held down, tap the letter **A** just once. The Applications window will appear.

2 Now that the Applications window is open and active, type the letter **T**.

This will select the first item in the Applications folder that starts with T, which should be TextEdit. (If not, hit the Tab key, which will select the next alphabetical item, *or* quickly type **TE**.)

3 Now that TextEdit is selected, use another keyboard shortcut to open it: Command O.

Or double-click the TextEdit icon.

TextEdit automatically opens a **blank document window,** ready for you to work.

> You will, at some point, open an application that doesn't automatically provide a blank window. In that case, just go to the File menu and choose "New."
>
> At some point you might also want to choose a new blank window when you've finished with one document and want to get started on another. You don't have to quit the application—just open a "New" document. You can have as many documents open at once as you like.

Open a blank document

The first time I went to the File menu to open a blank document, I saw the options **New** and **Open.** And I thought, "Well, I want to OPEN a NEW one." It confused me mightily. This is the difference:

New vs. Open

> NEW: Opens a blank, untitled, unsaved document.
>
> OPEN: Opens an existing document of your choice that has already been titled and saved. Perhaps you want to continue working on it or make changes.

Exercise 2: Type.

1 One quick thing before you start typing: Go to the "Format" menu in TextEdit and look for the command "Wrap to Page." If you find it, choose it (if not, skip to Step 2). The "Wrap to Page" option displays your page closer to what it will look like when you print it.

This is called "Wrap to Page."

2 Just start typing. Type at least a paragraph, *ignoring typos for now.*

At the ends of lines, **do not** hit the Return key—the text, as you type, will bump into the far-right edge and bounce back to the left side automatically.

3 **Do** hit the Return key at the end of a paragraph. Hit it twice if you want a double space between your paragraphs.

4 Go to the next page in this book and read about the **insertion point** and the **I-beam,** then continue with the exercises.

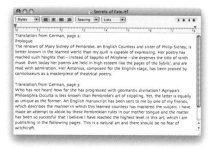

This is called "Wrap to Window."

I-beam

You may already be familiar with the Macintosh word processing **I-beam** (pronounced eye-beam). It looks like this (or very similar): ⌶

The tiny crossbar just below the center of the I-beam indicates the "baseline" of type, the invisible line that type sits upon.

On the Mac, the I-beam is a **visual clue** that you are now in a typing mode, as opposed to seeing an arrow or a crosshair or any number of other "cursors" that appear in various applications.

- *The I-beam is simply another pointer.* And just like the pointer, it doesn't do anything until you click it or press-and-drag it.

Insertion point

When you move the I-beam pointer to a spot within text and *single-click,* it sets down a flashing **insertion point** that looks like this: | (but it flashes).

This insertion point is extremely important! First you click the mouse to *set* the insertion point, then you *move the I-beam* out of the way (using the mouse)—**the insertion point is what you need to begin typing,** not the I-beam!!

The I-beam merely positions the insertion point.

With the insertion point flashing, anything you type will start at that point and move out to the right. This is true whether the insertion point is at the beginning or the end of a paragraph, in the middle of a word, in a field of a dialog box, in the name of an icon at your Desktop, or anywhere else.

Note: The only time the words will not move to the right in a word processor is if the text is centered or flush right, as described on page 71, or if you've set a tab other than left-aligned.

If you noticed, when you first opened a new, blank document in TextEdit, there was an insertion point flashing in the upper-left corner, indicating you could start typing immediately.

At any time you can use the mouse to move the I-beam pointer somewhere else in the existing text, click to set an insertion point, move the I-beam out of the way, and start typing from the new insertion point.

To type below the existing text, set the insertion point directly after the last character in the text, then hit the Return key a number of times until the insertion point is where you want to begin typing.

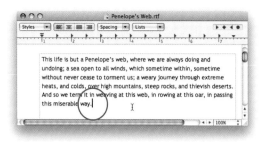

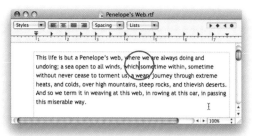

Do you see the insertion point at the end of the paragraph? If I start to type again in this story, it will begin at that insertion point.

The I-beam (do you see it?) is just hanging around waiting to be useful.

Do you see where I moved the insertion point to? If I start to type again in this story, the new text will begin at that insertion point.

Do you see the I-beam?

Exercise 3: Learn to be conscious of the I-beam and the insertion point.

1 Type a few more letters on your page. Notice how the **insertion point** moves *in front* of the characters as you type.

2 Stop typing. Move the mouse around, and notice that the cursor is not a pointer, but an **I-beam.**

   (The cursor becomes a pointer when you move off of the word processing page, but when you position it over the text, it becomes the I-beam.)

3 Using your mouse:
   • Position that I-beam anywhere in your paragraph,
      … single-click,
      … shove the mouse (and thus the I-beam) out of the way,
      … and start typing.

   Notice the insertion point moves to where you click the I-beam, and your new typing starts at that point.

4 Single-click the I-beam at the very end of the existing text—this will set the insertion point there. Now it's ready for you to continue typing.

65

Delete
(or Backspace)

When you press the **Delete** key (found in the upper-right of the main part of the keyboard), it deletes anything **to the left of the insertion point.**

You can backspace/delete to **correct typos** (typographical errors) as you type, *or* you can click to set the insertion point down anywhere else in your text and backspace from that new position.

After you make a correction and you want to continue typing at the end of your story, single-click the I-beam at the end of the story to set the insertion point there, then type.

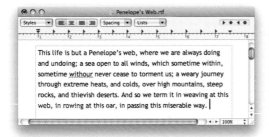

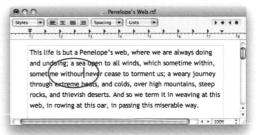

This paragraph has a typo. Do you see it? TextEdit has underlined the typo with red dots. I need to go back and fix it.

I used the I-beam to set the insertion point just to the **right** of the typo. Now I can hit the Delete key to erase that wrong letter and type the correct one in its place.

Delete characters

Exercise 4: Edit your text.

1 In the text on your page, notice where the insertion point is flashing.

2 Hit the **Delete** key several times. Watch as it deletes the characters **to the left** of the insertion point.

3 Now, using your mouse:

• Position that I-beam anywhere in your paragraph,

… single-click,

… shove the mouse (and I-beam) out of the way,

… and hit the Delete key one or more times.

Notice TextEdit deletes text to the left of the insertion point. Every Mac program will do the same thing.

4 Using the mouse, position the I-beam **at the end** of your text.

5 Click to set the insertion point (then move the mouse/ I-beam out of the way) so you can start typing again from the end of your document.

You've probably noticed that TextEdit puts **red dots** under words that it thinks are **misspelled.** If the word is *not* misspelled, you can just ignore the red dots—they won't print. But if you want to fix a typo, here's a great trick (and it works in Mail, too):

1   Hold down the Control key and single-click anywhere in the misspelled word. This makes a contextual menu pop up, like the ones you used in Chapter 5.

2   TextEdit provides a list of possible words, based on the misspelled word. If you see the correct spelling, single-click on it and the typo is corrected; if you don't see the correct spelling, click anywhere on the page and make the correction yourself.

If you don't see a list of possible words, it means the word is spelled correctly.

What?! **One space after a period?** If you grew up on a typewriter, this is a difficult habit to change, I know. Or if you were taught keyboarding skills by someone who grew up on a typewriter, they taught you typewriter rules. But characters on a Macintosh are not *monospaced* as they are on a typewriter (except for a few typefaces such as Monaco, Courier, and Andale Mono), so there is no need to use two spaces to separate two sentences. Check any book or magazine on your shelf; you will never find two spaces after periods (except publications produced on a computer typed by someone still using typewriter rules).

If you find this hard to accept, read *The Mac is not a typewriter.* It's a very little book. If you're interested in creating fine typography, read *The Non-Designer's Type Book.* Yes, I wrote them.

For the ultimate authority, check the question-and-answer page on the web site for the *Chicago Manual of Style:*

www.ChicagoManualOfStyle.org

One space after periods

If you do or don't want TextEdit to check your spelling as you type, go to the Edit menu and slide down to "Spelling."

In the hierarchical menu, a checkmark next to "Check Spelling as You Type" means it **will** check your spelling. If there is no checkmark, it **won't.**

Choose the command to put a checkmark there **or** to remove the existing checkmark, depending on what you want it to do.

If the application thinks a word is misspelled but it's a real word, like a name, choose the "Learn Spelling" option in the menu shown to the left.

See Chapter 10 for details on how to go to a web page.

Select (highlight) text

When you **select text,** it becomes **highlighted.** Once text is selected, you can do things to it, such as change its size, the type-face, delete it, etc.

If you use the I-beam to double-click on a word anywhere on the Mac, the entire word is selected, indicated by the highlighting.

This <mark>word</mark> is highlighted. I double-clicked on the word to select it.

To select more than one word, *press-and-drag* over the entire area you wish to highlight. <mark>This entire sentence is highlighted.</mark>

To select all of the text in an entire document, use the keyboard shortcut Command A.

Exercise 5: Experiment with selecting text.

1 In the paragraph you typed earlier, position the I-beam in the middle of any word.

2 **Double-click** on the word to select it. Try it on different words until you feel comfortable selecting whole words.

3 **Now select a range of text:**

- Position the I-beam somewhere toward the top of a paragraph,
    - … press the mouse button down and hold it down,
    - … then drag the mouse downward. (You can move up as well, or straight left or right, as long as you keep the mouse button down.)
- When you have a range of text selected, let go of the mouse button.
- Try it several times until you feel comfortable selecting a range of text.

To un-highlight (deselect) text, single-click anywhere, even in the highlighted space.

Once a word is selected (highlighted), anything you type will **entirely replace the selected text.** That is, you don't have to hit the Delete key first to get rid of the text—just type. This is true everywhere on the Mac.

Exercise 6: *Delete* **selected text, and also** *replace* **selected text with new text.**

1 In the paragraph you typed earlier, use the I-beam to double-click on a word to select it.

2 Hit the **Delete** key once to delete the selected word. Do this several times until it feels very comfortable.

3 Now, double-click a word to select it, *or* press-and-drag to select a range of text.

4 *Do not* hit the Delete key this time: just type a new word and watch it **replace** the selected text.

5 Try selecting a range of text and while it is highlighted, type a new sentence. Repeat until it feels comfortable.

Try these tips for **moving the insertion point** and for **selecting text** anywhere on the Mac:

Extra tips

- Use the arrow keys to move the insertion point backward and forward, up and down.

- Hold down the Shift key as you hit the arrow keys, and the text will be *selected* along the way. Try it.

- Triple-click in the middle of a sentence to select the entire paragraph. (In some applications, a triple-click will select one single line instead of the entire paragraph).

- This is my favorite selection trick:
    - **Single-click** at the point where you want to begin the selection; the insertion point will flash,

        …move the I-beam to where you want the selection to end (don't drag with the mouse button down and don't click anything yet!),

        …hold down the Shift key,

        …**Single-click** where you want the selection to end.

    I call this the Click Shift-Click Trick.

TextEdit allows you to select discontiguous text! That is, you can select one word or line or paragraph, then hold down the Command-key and drag to add other text that is not contiguous.

Change fonts (typefaces) and type size

Throughout the entire Mac environment, to make any changes to anything you must follow this rule, Rule No. 2:

Select First, Then Do It.

For instance, **to change text to a different font,** or typeface:

1 First you'll *select* the characters you want to change.

2 Then you'll *choose* the font that you want to apply to the text.

Exercise 7: Add a headline to your text, and then change the headline font.

1 First **add a headline** at the beginning of the paragraph you typed earlier. To do that:

With the mouse, move the I-beam to the beginning of the text; position it to the *left* of the very first letter.

Single-click at that position to set the insertion point. If you miss and the insertion point is a letter or two to the right or perhaps on the next line down, use the arrow keys to move the insertion point to the very beginning of the first line.

Tip: To see what each font looks like, click the "Action" button in the bottom-left of the Font window (the gear shift button), and from its menu choose "Show Preview." Each font and size you select will appear in the preview.

2 Type a headline of some sort, something like *My Important Headline.* The existing text will move along to the right as you type the new headline.

3 At the end of your headline, hit Return twice.

4 Now **select the headline:** Starting at one end or the other of the headline, press-and-drag over the text so you select every character. (Or triple-click in the line.)

5 Now that the headline is selected, go to the Format menu, choose "Font," then "Show Fonts." You'll see the dialog box shown below.

6 Select a font from the "Family" column, then a typeface style from the "Typeface" column, then a size from the "Size" column (or type a number). Voilà!

Drag the title bar to move the Fonts palette.

Choose a font name from the "Family" list.

Then choose one of the available "Typeface" styles (different fonts have different styles).

Then choose a font "Size."

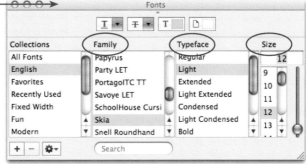

Alignment

Alignment refers to where the text is lined up.

> **Align left:** Text is lined up on the *left* side, and the right is "ragged," as shown in these short lines.

> **Align right:** Text is lined up
> on the *right*, and
> the left edge is ragged.
> This is also known as *flush right.*

> **Align center:**
> Text is centered on a vertical axis
> *between your margins.*
> If you change your margins,
> your centered text
> will shift.

> **Justified***:* Text is lined up on both the left *and* right margins, as seen in this short paragraph.

To change your alignment, you know what to do! That's right: *select first, then do it*—highlight the text, then choose the alignment from the buttons, as shown below, or from the menu commands (under the "Format" menu, choose "Text" and you'll see the alignment options).

Alignment buttons: align left, center, justified, and right.

Use this menu to change the spacing between selected lines.

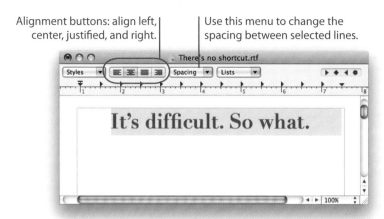

In this example, you can see that the text is selected (highlighted) and the center alignment button is checked.

Tip: When you plan to change the alignment, you don't have to select every character in the line or paragraph—to select an entire paragraph, just single-click in it. The paragraph will not be *highlighted,* but it will be *selected.* Try it.

71

Cut, Copy, and the Clipboard

Almost anywhere you can type, you can cut or copy text.

When you **cut** text (or a graphic), it is **removed** from your document and placed on the "Clipboard."

When you **copy** text (or a graphic), the original text is **intact** in your document and a *copy* of it is placed on the Clipboard.

Well, what the heck is a Clipboard?

The **Clipboard** is an invisible "container" somewhere in the depths of the Mac. It temporarily holds whatever you have cut or copied, be it text, spreadsheet data, graphics, an entire folder, etc. Once something is on the Clipboard, it waits there until you **paste** it somewhere (we'll get to that in a minute).

The most important thing to remember about the Clipboard is that *it holds only one thing at a time*; that is, as soon as you cut or copy something else, whatever was in the Clipboard to begin with is replaced by the new selection.

In some programs, including the Finder, you'll find a menu command called "Show Clipboard," usually in the Edit menu. When you can see it, the Clipboard appears as a window with its contents displayed, as shown below. In most programs, though, you never see the actual Clipboard—you have to simply trust it.

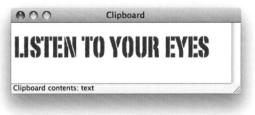

The Clipboard appears as a window (if it's available for looking at in your program). No matter where you copied or cut an item from, you can always go to the Finder's Edit menu and show the Clipboard to see what you've got.

Items will stay on the Clipboard even when you change applications: you can put a paint image on the Clipboard in a paint program, then open a word processing document and paste the paint image into a letter.

Items will disappear from the Clipboard when the computer is turned off or if there is a power failure, so don't count on keeping something in the Clipboard for very long!

How to Cut: Select first, then do it. Remember, whatever you cut **Cut** will *disappear* from the document.

The text is selected and ready to be cut.

The text has been cut. All that's left is the insertion point.

Exercise 8: Cut some text.

1. Select the text you wish to remove from the document (press-and-drag over the text).

2. From the Edit menu, choose "Cut."

   The text will be *eliminated* from your document and placed on the Clipboard. Now you can paste it somewhere; see the following pages.

If you want to undo the cut you just made, go to the Edit menu and choose "Undo Cut."

Be sure to read about the differences between "Cut" and "Clear" or "Delete" on page 78.

Copy   **How to Copy:** Select first, then do it.

This text is selected, ready to be copied.

The text has been copied, and it looks like nothing happened because the text is still there. That's exactly what it's supposed to do.

So the copied text is on the Clipboard. Now what? Well, the Clipboard holds objects for *pasting*. You can take text or a graphic out of one place and paste it into your document somewhere else, just as if you had a little glue pot. We'll get to that in just a moment (next page).

Exercise 9: Copy some text.

1   Select the text you wish to copy.

2   From the Edit menu, choose "Copy."

The text will *remain* in your document and a *copy* will be placed on the Clipboard. Now you can paste it in the next exercise.

Paste

How to Paste: When you go to the Edit menu and choose "Paste," you need to know *where* it will paste.

- Whatever was on the Clipboard will be inserted in your document *beginning at the flashing insertion point.* So if you want the pasted item to appear at a certain place in your document, **first** click the I-beam to position the insertion point.

- If you have a *range of text selected,* the pasted item will *replace* what was selected.

As long as something is on the Clipboard, you can paste it a million times in many different applications.

In other types of applications, like drawing and painting applications, a pasted object will usually just land in the middle of the page.

Exercise 10: **Paste some text.**

1 Because you previously cut or copied some text, you know there is text on the Clipboard waiting to be pasted. (If you didn't do Exercise 8 or 9, do one of them now so you have something on the Clipboard.)

2 Using the mouse, *position the I-beam* where you want to paste in the text, then *click* to set the insertion point.

3 Go to the Edit menu and choose "Paste." The text will be pasted in beginning at that insertion point.

On the following page is an example of each step in the cut-and-paste process.

And then:

4 Repeat Steps 2 and 3 (above) several more times. Notice you can keep pasting in the same text over and over.

5 Cut or copy some *other* text, then repeat Steps 2 and 3 above. Notice you are now pasting the *other* text.

Exercise 11: **Cut a paragraph and paste it somewhere else.**

1 Type several paragraphs on your page, if you haven't already.

2 Change the formatting of the first paragraph so it looks very different: change the font, the typeface style, and the size.

3 Triple-click anywhere in the formatted paragraph to select the entire paragraph.

4 Use the keyboard shortcut to cut the selected paragraph: Command X.

5 Set the insertion point at the end of your text and hit two Returns.

6 Press Command V (the keyboard shortcut) to paste the paragraph in, starting at the insertion point.

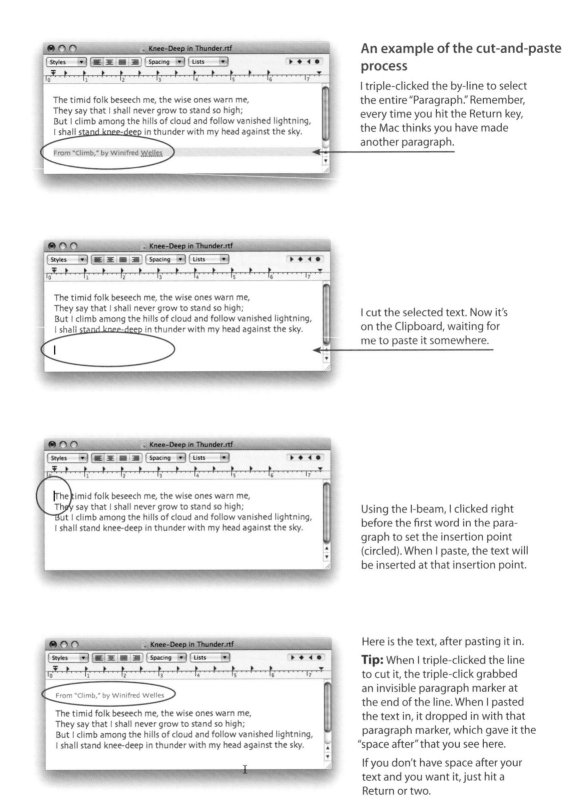

An example of the cut-and-paste process

I triple-clicked the by-line to select the entire "Paragraph." Remember, every time you hit the Return key, the Mac thinks you have made another paragraph.

I cut the selected text. Now it's on the Clipboard, waiting for me to paste it somewhere.

Using the I-beam, I clicked right before the first word in the paragraph to set the insertion point (circled). When I paste, the text will be inserted at that insertion point.

Here is the text, after pasting it in.

Tip: When I triple-clicked the line to cut it, the triple-click grabbed an invisible paragraph marker at the end of the line. When I pasted the text in, it dropped in with that paragraph marker, which gave it the "space after" that you see here.

If you don't have space after your text and you want it, just hit a Return or two.

Exercise 12: Copy a heading from one document and paste it into another document.

1 On the page you've been working with, type something like a headline. Format it (choose a font, typeface style, and size).

2 Select the text you just formatted.

3 Either cut or copy the selected text.

4 Open a new TextEdit window: Go to the File menu and choose "New" (or use the keyboard shortcut Command N).

5 In the new window (which is a new document), type a few lines.

6 Set the insertion point and paste—the headline you formatted and copied from the other document is now in this new document.

Undo

Undo can sometimes save your boompah (no, that's not computer jargon—it's Grandma's euphemism).

When you do something that makes you scream, "Aack! Oh no!" try Undo. It's always the first command in the Edit menu (or press Command Z).

Important Note: What Undo can undo is *only the last action that occurred.* For instance, if you selected two paragraphs of brilliantly witty text that you spent three hours composing and then the cat walked across your keyboard and obliterated the entire work, Undo could give it back to you **IF** you Undo before you touch *anything.* Don't start fiddling around with the keys and the mouse because then what you will undo is that fiddling around.

So if something goes wrong, don't scream—**UNDO.**

Then scream.

(Some applications, such as illustration programs and page layout applications, can Undo multiple times. Check your manual.)

Keyboard shortcuts

In Chapter 5 you learned how to use keyboard shortcuts for various tasks. Thoughtfully, the **keyboard shortcuts** for the Undo, Cut, Copy, and Paste commands are very handy. Notice on your keyboard the letters **Z, X, C,** and **V,** all lined up in a row right above the Command key—these are the shortcut keys.

Remember, select first (*except to Undo*); then hold down the Command key and lightly tap the letter.

Command **Z** will Undo	Z is very close to the Command key.
Command **X** will Cut	X like Xing it out.
Command **C** will Copy	C for Copy.
Command **V** will Paste	V because it is next to C; it's sort of like the caret symbol ^ for inserting.

Delete or Clear and the Clipboard

Now, the **Delete** key (on the upper-right of the main group of keys) works a little differently from the Cut command:

Delete: If you hit the Delete key while something is selected, whatever is selected is *deleted* but is *not* placed on the Clipboard.

This means if you are holding something in the Clipboard to paste in again, whatever you delete from your document will *not* replace what you are currently holding in the Clipboard.

But it also means that you don't have that deleted item anymore—*whatever you delete is really gone and cannot be pasted anywhere* (but remember, you can Undo!).

Clear, in the Edit menu, does the same thing as the Delete key.

Access special characters

Special characters are the symbols you have access to on the Macintosh that weren't available on typewriters, such as upside-down question marks for Spanish (¿), the pound symbol for English money (£), the cents sign (¢), the registration or trademark symbols (® ™), the copyright symbol (©), etc.

Below is a short list of special characters you can experiment with. For each character, hold down the modifier key (Option, Shift, etc.) and tap the character key noted. For instance, to type a bullet, hold down the Option key and tap the number 8 on the top of your keyboard (not the number 8 on the keypad). It's no different from typing an asterisk, where you hold down the Shift key and tap the 8.

•	bullet	Option 8
©	copyright	Option G
™	trademark	Option 2
®	registration	Option R
¢	cents	Option $
€	euro	Option Shift 2
°	degree	Option Shift 8
…	ellipsis	Option ;
–	en dash	Option Hyphen
—	em dash	Option Shift Hyphen

Use real accent marks

You can type **accent marks** on the Mac, as in résumé and piñata. It's easy to remember that you use the Option key, and the accents are hiding beneath the keyboard characters that would usually be under them. For example, the acute accent over the **é** is **Option e;** the tilde over the **ñ** is **Option n.**

Exercise 13: To type accent marks, follow these steps (using the word Résumé):

1 Type the word until you come to the letter that will be *under* the accent mark; e.g., **R**

2 *Before* you type that next letter (the letter **e** in this case), type the Option combination (**Option e** in this case, which means hold down the Option key and tap the **e** once)—*it will look like nothing happened.* That's okay.

3 Now let go of the Option key. Type the character that is to be *under* the accent mark. Both the mark and the letter will appear together; e.g., **R é**

4 Type the rest of the word: **R é s u m é**

5 Now try typing **Voilà!**

Here is a list of common accent marks:

´	Option e
`	Option ~
¨	Option u
~	Option n
^	Option i

79

Document windows

Document windows are very similar to Finder windows, but they do have a few differences.

You can tell the window below is a **document window** because in the menu bar across the top of the monitor, just to the right of the apple, is the name of the application in which this document is being created. Pages, a program from Apple, is a word processing/page layout application—much more powerful than TextEdit, and a fabulous alternative to Microsoft Word.

Mariner Write is another great word processing application. www.MarinerSoftware.com

Document windows have no Sidebars, but they often have their own Toolbars with buttons and options appropriate to the specific application.

This is the name of the application whose window is active.

This is the name, or **title,** of the document I have created in this application (you'll name yours in the next chapter).

Every document you create will be in its own window.

You can see that the biggest difference between this window and a Finder window is that there is no "Sidebar" on the side.

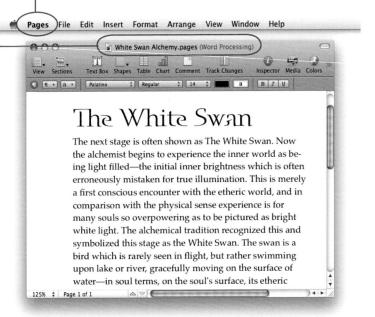

Just like any Finder window, you can **resize** a document window by dragging its resize corner (bottom-right), **move** it by dragging the title bar, **scroll** through it by dragging a blue scroller or the tiny triangles in the corner, and **close** it by clicking in the red button. Check it out.

Double-Return: Hitting the Return key twice creates a double space between the lines. This is for extra space between individual paragraphs.

If you want the **entire document,** or even just a piece of it, **double-spaced**—that's different: In TextEdit, select all (press Command A) *or* select the paragraphs you want double-spaced. Single-click the "Spacing" button in the Toolbar, then choose "Double."

Eventually you'll want to learn how to create an automatic increase of space between paragraphs instead of using a double-Return. Check the manual for your software or check its Help files.

Remove a Return: The computer sees a Return as just another character, which means to *remove* a Return you simply backspace over it with the Delete key, just as you would to remove an unwanted character. The problem is that in most programs you can't *see* the Return character. Just set the insertion point to the *left* of the first character on the line, then Delete, as shown:

> Let's say I'm typing away and my dog shoves her big head under my arm and suddenly
>
> my text starts typing on the wrong line, like this. What to do?

Set the insertion point directly to the *left* of the text that's on the wrong line (as shown below).

> Let's say I'm typing away and my dog shoves her big head under my arm and suddenly
>
> my text starts typing on the wrong line, like this. What to do?

Hit the Delete key to remove the empty line above that new, unwanted paragraph (*you* don't think it's a paragraph, but the computer does). Now it will look like this:

> Let's say I'm typing away and my dog shoves her big head under my arm and suddenly
> my text starts typing on the wrong line, like this. What to do?

Delete again to wrap the sentence back up to the one above.

> Let's say I'm typing away and my dog shoves her big head under my arm and suddenly my text starts typing on the wrong line, like this. What to do? Oh, it's all fixed!

Move the insertion back to where you want to begin typing.

Remember

- Use the **I-beam** only to move and set the **insertion point.** The insertion point is the important thing— that's where type will start typing, and that's where text will paste in.

- Only type **one space after periods** or any other punctuation.

- Cut, Copy, Paste, Undo, Clear, and Delete are the same all over the Mac, everywhere you go. The **keyboard shortcuts** are always the same.

Save & Print

7

You must **save your document** if you ever want to see it again. And of course you must **print it** if you want to see your work on paper.

This chapter uses the document you created in Chapter 6. If you didn't do those exercises, open a new TextEdit document and type several paragraphs so you can work with the exercises and experiments in this chapter.

Save your document

If you are new to computers, all you need to do is this **quick-and-easy save.** This will store your document in the Documents folder, which is in your Home area.

You don't have to wait until your document is finished before you save it. In fact, you should save and title it as soon as you start, and then keep saving the changes along the way, explained below. If you don't save regularly and something happens like the power goes out for a split second, you have lost forever whatever was not saved! **SOS:** Save Often, Sweetie!

Exercise 1: Save your document with a name, or title.

Tip: Give your document a title you will remember! A title like "Memo" is going to confuse you when you have a folder full of thirty memos.

1 Make sure the document you want to save is open and in front of you—single-click on it to make sure.

2 From the File menu, choose "Save As...." This will open the "Save As" dialog box, shown below.

3 Type the name of your file in the "Save As" field, as pointed out below.

Type the name of your document here.

This tells you the folder in which your document will be stored.

```
○ ○ ○                    Untitled

  Save As:  Untitled.rtf                    ▼

   Where:  📄 Documents              ⬍

  File Format:  Rich Text Format (RTF)      ⬍

                          Cancel    Save
```

4 Click the Save button (or hit the Return or Enter key).

You're all done! The Mac has saved your file into the Documents folder, as shown on the opposite page. Your document appears in front of you again so you can continue working on it.

From now on, press Command S **every few minutes** to **update** the new changes you've made as you work (you won't see a dialog box when you press Command S). This ensures that if something happens, you won't lose more than a couple of minutes of work.

If you want, you can skip to the printing part of this chapter now! (See page 87.)

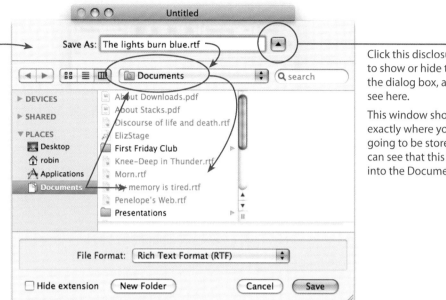

Click this disclosure triangle to show or hide the rest of the dialog box, as you can see here.

This window shows you exactly where your file is going to be stored—you can see that this file will go into the Documents folder.

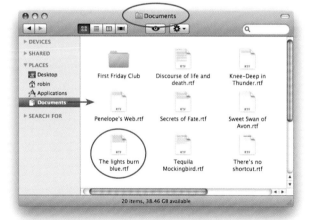

Once you have titled and saved a document, its icon appears in the folder in which you saved it, as shown above.

To open that document again, double-click the icon.

If you choose to view your Documents window in the List View or Column View, it will look like the one above. Do you see the new document?

85

Make several versions of the same document

Sometimes you might want to create changes in a document, but you still want to keep a **copy of the original without the changes.** For instance, let's say you write a witty letter to Uncle Jerry, then decide you also want to write to Uncle Floyd. You have a few things to tell Floyd that Jerry isn't interested in, but you don't want to retype the entire letter. That's when you'll use "Save As…" *a second time* to give the document *a new name,* which actually creates a new, separate file and leaves the original file intact.

Exercise 2: Make another version based on the original.

1 Create a new document (go to the File menu and choose "New," *or* press Command N). Type a few witty paragraphs in this new document

2 Save this original document and give it a name (as described on page 84). Let's say you've named it "Witty letter to Uncle Jerry." *Don't close the document.*

3 While that document is still open on the screen, from the File menu, choose "Save As…" *again.*

4 Change the name, say from "Witty letter to Uncle Jerry" to "Witty letter to Uncle Floyd."

This automatically puts the *original* document (to Uncle Jerry) safely away on your disk and *creates a new one* (the copy to Uncle Floyd) right on the screen. You'll notice the name in the title bar of your document changes to what you renamed it. *Any changes you make to this document (Uncle Floyd's) will not affect the original (Uncle Jerry's).*

Witty letter to Uncle
Jerry.pages

Witty letter to Uncle
Floyd.pages

Witty letter to Uncle
Merv.pages

Witty letter to Uncle
Jeff.pages

All of these letters are based on the original letter to Uncle Jerry. I just kept choosing "Save As" and giving the new ones new names. The information, layout, type choices, etc., all stayed the same, but now each letter is separate and I can add or delete details in each.

Print your document

Here are the briefest of directions for **printing your pages.** If it works, then you can skip the rest of this chapter, unless you want to understand what some of the options are. For this very quick start, make sure the printer is plugged into the wall *and* into the computer with the appropriate cables, there is paper in the printer, and the printer is turned on and warmed up (wait until it stops making noises). Then:

Exercise 3: Print your document.

1 Open the document that you want to print.

2 From the File menu, choose "Print...."

3 Click the "Print" button (or hit the Return key).

That's all. **If it worked,** skip to page 91 if you want to learn about some of the printing options.

If the "Printer" menu in the dialog box, circled below, says **"No Printer Selected,"** go to the next page and follow the directions to add your printer to the list. You only have to do this once and then printing will be as easy as the three steps above.

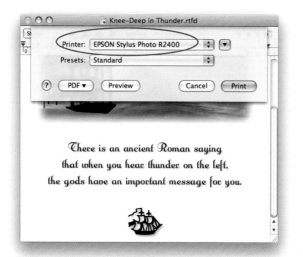

This is typically what you will see when you choose to Print. There are lots of settings that you won't see until you click the blue disclosure triangle, as explained on the following pages. But if you just want to print the pages in your document to make sure printing works, you can safely hit the "Print" button without bothering about anything else.

Tip: Do you see the button **"PDF ▾"**? If you click that and choose "Save as PDF…," your Mac will make a PDF file of this document for you, which is a special type of file that you can send to anyone on any kind of computer and it will look just like it does on your Mac. The other person doesn't need to have the fonts or applications you used or anything!

87

Add a printer to the list, if necessary

Your Mac needs to put your printer in its "Printer List" so you can choose to print to it and so the computer knows what that particular printer is capable of doing. For instance, if you print to an inexpensive color inkjet, the Print dialog box will provide color options, but probably not paper tray options. If you print to a color PostScript laser printer, you might have double-sided page options or larger paper sizes, for example.

To add a printer to the Printer List, you can either use the Print dialog box in your document (4a), **or** the Print & Fax system preferences (4b). Either method has the same result, as follows:

Exercise 4a: Use the Print dialog box to add a printer.

1 Turn on the printer you want to add to the list. Wait until it is fully warmed up (wait until it stops making noise and the green light is not flashing).

2 While your document is open, go to the File menu and choose "Print."

3 In the Print dialog box, click on the "Printer" menu and choose "Add Printer...," as shown below.

Go to Step 4 on the next page.

○ ○ ○   📄 Knee-Deep in Thunder.rtfd

Printer ✓ No Printer Selected	▼
Presets	**Add Printer...**
	Print & Fax Preferences...

(?) (PDF ▼) (Preview)   (Cancel) (Print)

Exercise 4b: Use the Print & Fax system preferences to add a printer.

1 Turn on the printer you want to add to the List. Wait until it is fully warmed up (wait until it stops making noise and the green light is not flashing).

2 From the Apple menu, choose "System Preferences...." Single-click the "Print & Fax" icon.

Print & Fax

3 On the left side, at the bottom of the "Printers" pane, click the **+** button to add a printer.

Go to Step 4 on the next page.

4 Both methods described on the previous page will open the printer list, as shown below. This list shows you the printers the Mac knows about already. Your Mac is aware of the most common printers and already has the "drivers" it needs to print to them.

However, if you bought some fancy or expensive printer, be sure to install the software that came with it before you try to add it or print to it.

5 Single-click the name of the printer you want to use, then click the "Add" button.

6 That printer is now added to the list and you will be able to choose it in the Print dialog box.

If you can't add a printer

Note: If you can't make your printer appear in the list, check that the printer is turned on and that the cables are connected tightly (check both ends of every cable).

If you haven't done so already, install the printer's software and restart your Mac.

If the printer is being shared from another Mac, make sure the other Mac is turned on and is not asleep.

Sometimes printer cables go bad; if you've checked everything else, try a new cable.

Check the web site of the printer vendor and download the necessary software, if they have it—have a knowledgeable friend help you, if you're not sure how to do it.

If you have a very new printer, perhaps it is not yet supported by Leopard. Check the vendor's web site.

89

Page setup

You should get in the habit of checking the **Page Setup** option in the File menu. Page Setup opens a dialog box where you can set specifications for printing the document—use these in conjunction with the individual Print dialog box specifications, as shown on the following pages. Below are sample Page Setup boxes, but your particular application may have other features of its own.

Discourse of life and death.rtf

Settings: Page Attributes

Format for: EPSON Stylus Photo R2400
Epson Stylus Photo R2400 – Guten...

Paper Size: US Letter
8.50 by 11.00 inches

Orientation:

Scale: 100 %

Cancel OK

If you have several printers in your list, use the "Format for" menu to choose the one you plan to print to so the Mac will find the specific details about it, like different paper sizes it can take, what kinds of color options, etc.

Click here for Help.

- **Paper Size:** This refers to the size of the paper that the document *will be printed on,* not the size of the page you are typing on. For instance, you might be creating a business card, but you can't put paper sized 2 x 3.5 through your printer—usually, the cards will be printed on regular letter-sized paper. If you have other-sized paper to use, choose it from this menu.

- **Orientation:** The Mac wants to know if the document should print normal (8.5 x 11) or sideways (11 x 8.5); also known as Tall or Wide, Portrait or Landscape.

- **Scale:** Enter a number here to enlarge or reduce the printed page. For instance, enter 50 % to print your work at half size. Remember, half of an 8.5 x 11 is 4.25 x 5.5—you must halve both directions. On paper, this looks like the image is ¼ the original size; it isn't—it's half of both the horizontal *and* the vertical.

Reducing an image reduces it in both directions, not just one.

90

Once you have successfully added your printer to the list, you can print merrily away. On these next few pages are explanations of the various printing options you have. You will see different print dialog boxes depending on which printer you are connected to, and the dialog boxes within different applications will look slightly different from what you see here, but basically all you need to do is answer the questions they ask.

Most applications have a special menu option for specifications particular to that application. For instance, below are the options for printing from TextEdit; you can see that your options are very different from those in Keynote, Apple's presentation application (a product much superior to PowerPoint).

Print specifications

Application-specific options

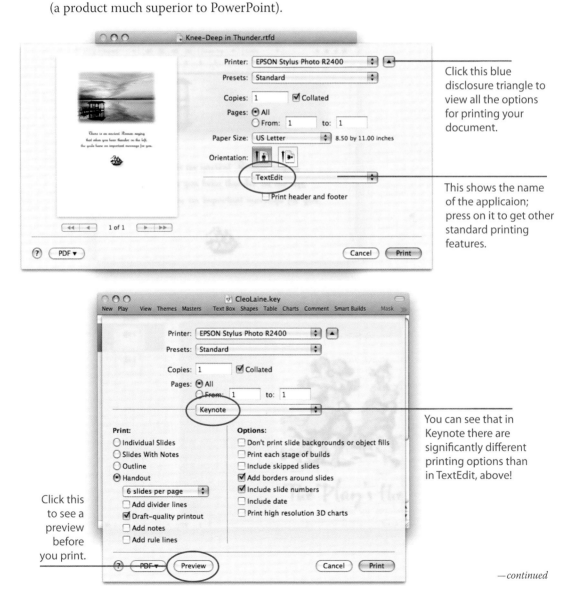

Click this blue disclosure triangle to view all the options for printing your document.

This shows the name of the applicaion; press on it to get other standard printing features.

You can see that in Keynote there are significantly different printing options than in TextEdit, above!

Click this to see a preview before you print.

—continued

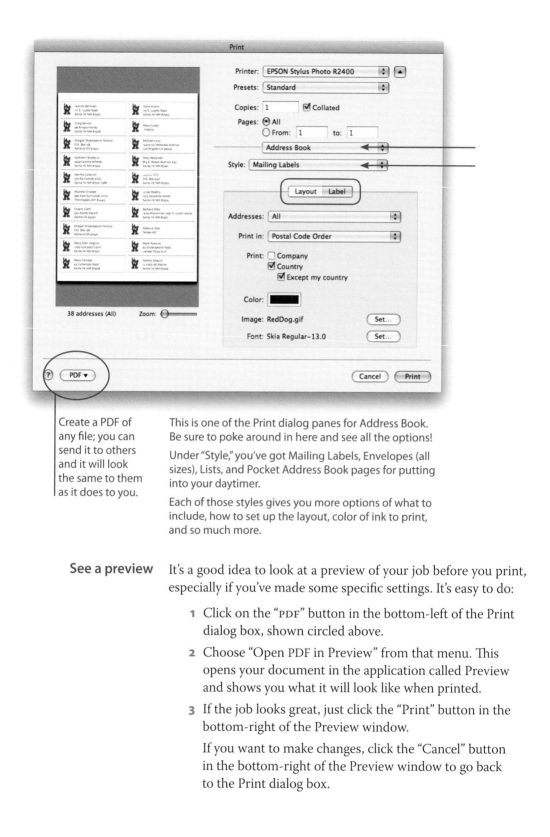

Create a PDF of any file; you can send it to others and it will look the same to them as it does to you.

This is one of the Print dialog panes for Address Book. Be sure to poke around in here and see all the options!

Under "Style," you've got Mailing Labels, Envelopes (all sizes), Lists, and Pocket Address Book pages for putting into your daytimer.

Each of those styles gives you more options of what to include, how to set up the layout, color of ink to print, and so much more.

See a preview   It's a good idea to look at a preview of your job before you print, especially if you've made some specific settings. It's easy to do:

1 Click on the "PDF" button in the bottom-left of the Print dialog box, shown circled above.

2 Choose "Open PDF in Preview" from that menu. This opens your document in the application called Preview and shows you what it will look like when printed.

3 If the job looks great, just click the "Print" button in the bottom-right of the Preview window.

If you want to make changes, click the "Cancel" button in the bottom-right of the Preview window to go back to the Print dialog box.

Very often you will not need to go beyond this first dialog box, where you can always choose **how many copies** to print and which **pages to print.**

- **Copies:** Type in the number of copies you want to print.

- **Collated:** If you're printing more than one copy of a multi-page document, you can make the printer collate the copies—it will print all the pages of one set, then print the next set. If you *don't* click collate, you will get, for instance, five copies of page 1, five copies of page 2, five copies of page 3, etc. Keep in mind that it takes a bit longer for the printer to collate than to print multiple copies of one page at a time.

- **Pages: All** or **From __ to __:** You can choose to print *all* of the pages contained in your document, or just pages 3 through 12 (or whatever your choice is, of course).

    If you want to print just page 3, for example, type 3 in both boxes.

    If you don't know the number of the last page, enter something like "999" and the printer will print to the end.

    Choose **All** to override any numbers in the **From/to** boxes.

    In this dialog box, you cannot print non-consecutive pages, such as pages 3, 7, and 11 (you'll have to print those pages individually). If you use a page layout or other more sophisticated application, you will have the option to print non-consecutive pages.

Layout   Choose **Layout** (from the menu circled below) when you want to print multiple pages on one sheet of paper. This is handy when you have, for instance, a presentation to give and you want to create handouts for your audience so they can follow along. Or it can help you see your overall project at a glance so you can get a better idea of how things are working together (or not).

In this example, I have chosen four pages per sheet, a layout direction of top to bottom, and a single hairline border around each individual miniature page.

- **Pages per Sheet:** Choose how many pages of your document you want to see on each printed sheet of paper. Every page will be reduced to fit, of course.

- **Layout Direction:** Click on a layout to determine how the pages are arranged on the sheet. In the example above, the third button is clicked.

- **Border:** Choose one of the four border options so each page will be clearly defined on the printed sheet.

You can only **print two-sided** (automatically) if you have bought a two-sided printer and installed its software. As you can see above, the option is grayed-out if your printer is not capable.

In **color inkjet printers,** the type of paper you specify and put in the printer makes a remarkable difference in the finished image. A low-quality mode with cheap paper makes an image look worse than in the newspaper comic strip. But photo-quality paper with a high-quality mode can make the same image look like a photograph you had enlarged at a photo studio. Use the **Print Settings** to specify the paper ("Media Type") you have ready in the printer, plus the quality of your finished product.

Print Settings

Your "Print Settings" might not look exactly like the ones shown. Read the manual for your particular printer to learn all the details about every option.

The chosen printer in this example is an Epson Stylus Photo R2400.

Go to the "Printer Features" to adjust the quality settings.

Some of the options will change as you choose different paper to print on and different quality.

Tips for printing photographs:

- Use "photo quality" paper.
- From the "Media Type" or "Paper Type" menu, choose the paper that best describes the type you put into the printer.
- Choose the highest quality printing option.

Your printer has a manual that will help you choose specifications for the best printing. Be sure to read it!

95

Using the print queue window

You have a **print queue window** for each printer that you have added to your Printer List. A "print queue" is a line up or sequence of jobs waiting to print. With this window you can control your print jobs, delete jobs, cancel them, queue them up for printing later, and more.

Control your print jobs

Below you see the print queue window where you manage your printing.

The name in the title bar of the window is the name of the printer that is printing these particular files. When this window (shown below) is visible, you have new menu items in the menu bar at the top of your monitor. The following describes things you can do using the menus or the icons in the toolbar.

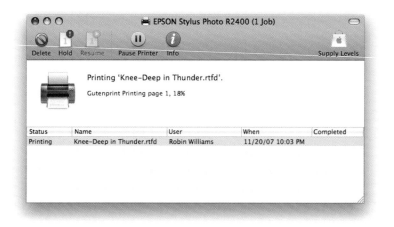

To display the window shown above.

1 As soon as you click the "Print" button, a printer icon appears on the right side of the Dock.

2 Single-click on that icon to get the printer job window shown above.

Also, see page 99 for a tip on how to get the printer job window at any time, even if you're not printing yet.

To control printing of individual documents and also of the entire printer:

- Single-click on the Printer icon in the Dock while your document is in the process of printing (as explained on the opposite page); this brings up the print queue window.

  If you tell a document to print and it doesn't print and you keep telling it to print over and over again, open this window and you'll see all of those documents waiting in line to print, just like you told them (see the next page).

  To fix things, first select the job names and click the "Delete" button, then figure out what's wrong: Is there one job clogging up the printer and the others are merely waiting, or have the jobs been stopped? (Read on.) When you have fixed the problem, print the piece again.

This tiny exclamation point means the print queue has been stopped or paused and your job will not print.

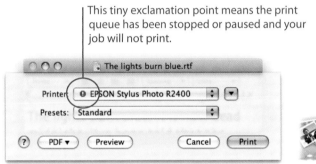

You'll also see a symbol on the printer icon in the Dock if the queue is on hold or paused.

- **STOP ONE JOB from printing:** In the print queue window, click once on the name of a document in the list, then click the "Hold" button (or go to the Jobs menu at the top of the screen and choose "Hold Job"). This does not *delete* the job from the queue—it just puts it on hold.

- **STOP ALL THE DOCUMENTS from printing:** If the jobs are in the process of printing, the icon in the toolbar is labeled "Pause Printer." Single-click it to stop the entire line-up of documents waiting to print. While it is stopped, you can delete jobs, print an individual job, go to lunch, etc.

—continued

If you try to print several times and nothing goes through, check to make sure the jobs have not been stopped! You'll know the queue has been stopped because the icon in the toolbar will be labeled "Resume Printer." Plus, if you see an exclamation point in the Print dialog box, as shown on the previous page, that means the queue has been stopped.

- **RESUME printing one job:** If a job has been put on hold, select its name in the job window. Then click the "Resume" button (or go to the Jobs menu and choose "Resume Job").

- **START ALL THE DOCUMENTS to print:** If the queue has been stopped, the icon in the toolbar is labeled "Resume Printer," as shown below. Single-click this icon to start the printing process for the entire line-up of documents. Or select one or more documents, go to the Jobs menu, and choose "Resume Job."

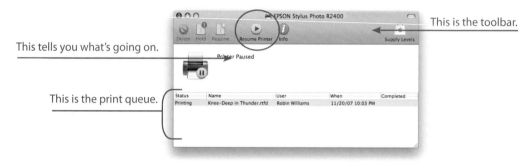

This is the toolbar.

This tells you what's going on.

This is the print queue.

- **CANCEL a print job:** In the print queue window, click once on a document name to select it, then hit the Delete button in the toolbar (or go to the Jobs menu and choose "Delete Job").

  You can select more than one job to delete: hold down the Command key and click on each document name you want to delete.

- **CREATE A QUEUE:** If you want to send a bunch of print jobs to the printer, but you don't want to print them right now, put them in a queue: First open the print queue window and click the icon to "Pause Printer." Then, in your application, send as many jobs as you like to print. Each one will tell you that printing has been stopped and ask if you want to put this job in the queue. Click "Add to Queue."

  Later, when you're ready, click the button to "Resume Printer" (or use the Dock menu, as shown to the left) and they will all print one after the other.

While you're printing, a **printer icon** appears in the **Dock,** then disappears when the job is finished. If you print regularly, though, it comes in handy to have the printer more easily accessible—you can keep it permanently in the Dock.

Keep your printer icon in the Dock

One way to make the icon stay in your Dock is to wait until the next time you print. You'll see the icon in the Dock. While it's there, *press* on it (don't click!) and you'll get the menu shown below. Choose "Keep in Dock," and the printer utility will stay there even after the printing is done.

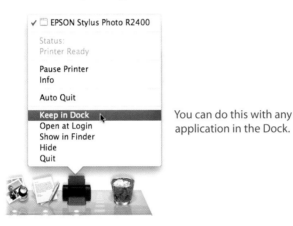

You can do this with any application in the Dock.

If you don't want to wait until next time you print, you can open the print queue window at any time through the System Preferences:

1 From the Apple menu, open "System Preferences...."

2 Single-click the "Print & Fax" icon.

3 Choose a printer from the left-hand pane.

4 Click the button to "Open Print Queue...."

The entire "Save As" dialog box

If you want to know all about the **Save As dialog box** and how to use it, read on. It will give you more control over where you are saving files. It's not as scary as it looks.

- **Name** your document **(1),** just as you have been doing.
- Your document will be **saved** into whichever folder or disk is shown in the **Save As menu (2),** which in the example on the opposite page is the Documents folder. *This is the most important thing to notice and remember!*
- You see the Documents folder is selected in the Sidebar **(3),** and the **contents** of the Documents folder **(4)** are shown in the column or directory pane to its right.
- This tells you that, as it is right now, your saved file will be saved and stored **inside** the Documents folder.
- **To save into a different folder,** single-click any folder name in either the Sidebar or the directory pane **(4)** to **select that folder.** That folder name will appear in the Save As menu at the top and its contents in the pane. If you then click the Save button **(5),** your file will be saved into *that* folder.

Do you see the button labeled "New Folder" at the bottom of the Save As dialog box? If you single-click that button, you can name a new folder and then when you click the Save button, your new document will be saved into *that* folder.

Type here to **name** or **title** the document. The highlight across the name is a **visual clue** telling you that this current name, "Untitled," is **selected**—just type, and this highlighted text will be replaced (that is, you don't have to delete the existing text first).

If you don't see the directory pane below, as shown here, click this disclosure triangle.

Choose the view in which you want to see the pane.

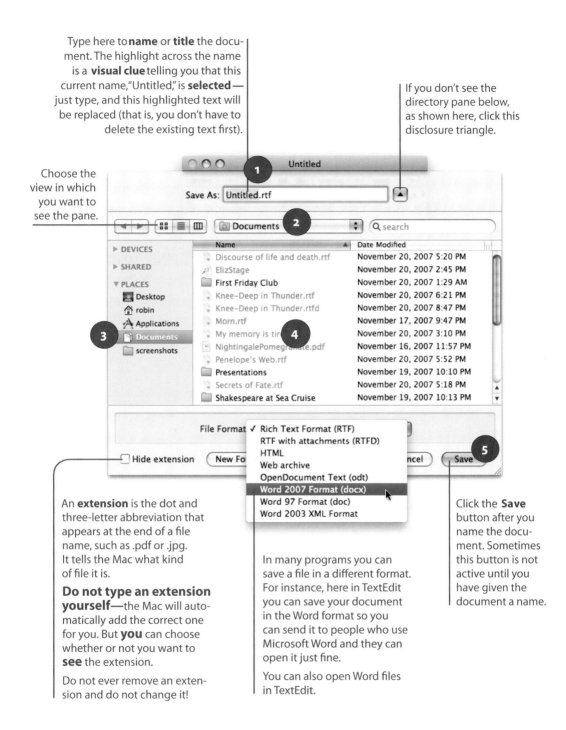

An **extension** is the dot and three-letter abbreviation that appears at the end of a file name, such as .pdf or .jpg. It tells the Mac what kind of file it is.

Do not type an extension yourself—the Mac will automatically add the correct one for you. But **you** can choose whether or not you want to **see** the extension.

Do not ever remove an extension and do not change it!

In many programs you can save a file in a different format. For instance, here in TextEdit you can save your document in the Word format so you can send it to people who use Microsoft Word and they can open it just fine.

You can also open Word files in TextEdit.

Click the **Save** button after you name the document. Sometimes this button is not active until you have given the document a name.

101

- **Save your document** with a memorable name as soon as you start working on it.

- **SOS:** Save Often, Sweetie! Use the keyboard shortcut (Command S) to save every few minutes.

  sos is Rule Number One on the Mac.

- If you keep sending a job to print and **nothing comes out,** check the printer job window—the jobs are probably on hold or they are just waiting for a slow job to finish printing. See pages 97–98.

Close, Quit & Trash

There are three tasks you will constantly repeat while working on your Mac: You will **close documents** you have created or opened; you will **quit applications;** and you'll **trash files** you don't need anymore. Each task is incredibly easy.

This chapter uses the document you saved in Chapter 7. If you didn't do those exercises, open a new TextEdit document and type several paragraphs so you can work with the exercises in this chapter.

Close vs. Quit

At first it seems a bit confusing—what's the big deal, **quitting** or **closing.** Either way, you're finished, right? Wrong.

Essentially, this is what happens: Say you open an *application* like your word processor—that is comparable to putting a typewriter on your office desk. Then you start a new *document*—that is comparable to putting a piece of paper in the typewriter.

When you choose "Close" from the File menu, that is comparable to taking the piece of paper (the document) out of the typewriter. The typewriter, though (the application), is still on the desk! On a computer, both the desk and the "typewriter" are rather invisible so you might think the typewriter (the application) is gone.

But the typewriter—the word processor—stays on the desk (in the computer's memory, called RAM) until you physically put the word processor away. When you choose "Quit" from the File menu, that is comparable to putting the typewriter away.

Now, since you're using Mac OS X, you don't have to worry about memory because OS X takes care of managing it. You can leave lots of applications open for days at a time, but you should still **save** those documents!

If you plan to edit movies or huge photos, you'll need more memory than what comes with a Mac (more memory can be added at any time). But if all you're doing is word processing and sending email and surfing the web, the amount that comes with the machine is probably fine for a long time.

Note: A gigabyte is 1024 megabytes, and a megabyte is 1024 kilobytes, and a kilobyte is 1024 bytes, and it takes 1 byte to make a standard character on the screen, like the letter "A."

And because I know you're dyin' to know, 1 byte is made of 8 bits.

And that's as small as it gets.

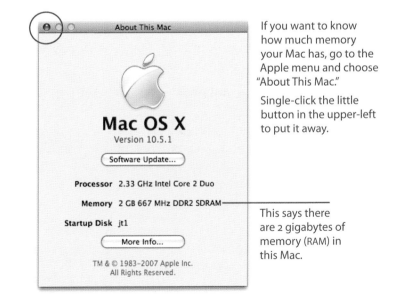

If you want to know how much memory your Mac has, go to the Apple menu and choose "About This Mac."

Single-click the little button in the upper-left to put it away.

This says there are 2 gigabytes of memory (RAM) in this Mac.

If a document window has a dot in the middle of the red button, that means it has **unsaved changes,** meaning you made changes to the document since the last time you saved it (if ever). Perhaps you wrote more, fixed a typo, or changed the typeface. If you don't save those changes before you close, you'll get a message warning you, as shown on page 108.

Unsaved changes

When the red Close button has a dot in it, that means you have made changes to it that aren't saved yet.

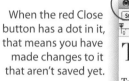

Exercise 1: **Save your document.**

Because Rule Number One on the Mac is "Save Often, Sweetie," (sos) let's just make sure the document you're working on is **saved.** If you don't have a document open, create a new one in TextEdit, as explained in Chapter 6.

1 Look at the red Close button on your document window. Is there a dot inside of it? That means, as you know by now, that the latest changes haven't been saved.

   If there is no dot in the middle, type another word and you'll see the dot appear.

2 Save it right now: just press Command S. You'll see the dot go away.

   You always want to save a document before you close it. In fact, press Command S to save your document every few minutes.

105

Close a document

When you are finished working on a document for the moment, you can **close that document window** in a number of ways:

- **Either** click the red button in the upper-left corner of the document window.
- **Or** choose "Close" from the File menu.
- **Or** in most applications, the keyboard shortcut to close a document is usually **Command W,** just like closing a Finder **w**indow.

Whichever method you use, you are simply closing the *document* window (putting away the paper) and the *application* (the software program) is still open. You still see the menu belonging to the application, even though the rest of your screen may look just like your Desktop, and you might even see windows that belong to other applications or to the Desktop!

Exercise 2: Close your document and open another.

1 Single-click on the document window just to make sure it's the active window.

2 Do any one of the three options listed above. Don't click anywhere else yet!

   If you have more than one document open, close the other one(s).

3 Notice even though the document window is gone, the menu bar across the top of the screen still says "TextEdit" (see the opposite page). That's because you closed the *document,* but you are still in the *application.*

4 Single-click anywhere on the Desktop.

5 Look at the menu bar now—where it said "TextEdit" a second ago, it should say "Finder" now. That's because as soon as you clicked on the Desktop, you popped out of the application TextEdit, and now the Finder/Desktop is active.

6 **Go back to TextEdit:** Notice the TextEdit icon in the Dock has a blue bubble beneath it; that's because it's still open, even though you can't see it.

   Single-click on the TextEdit icon and your menu bar will change to show that you are now in TextEdit.

7 **Create a new document** in TextEdit: From the "File" menu, choose "New."

   Type a paragraph or two, and save it into the Documents folder with the name "Toss This" because you're going to throw it away soon.

You can tell by the menu bar that TextEdit is the active application.

Notice there are **two windows open,** a document window and a Finder window. The document window is "active"; you can tell because the three buttons in the upper-left are in color.

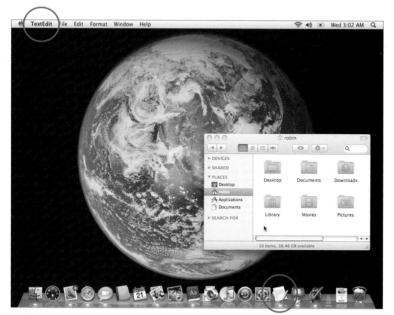

Even though I closed the document, TextEdit is still active—you can see its name in the menu bar.

If I were to single-click on the Finder window (which is gray at the moment because it is **not** active), that Finder window would "come forward" and be active, and the menu bar would change to "Finder" instead of "TextEdit."

Quit an application

To quit an application, you must choose the Quit command. This command is always in the application menu (the one with the name of the current application), and "Quit" is always the very last item. In every application you can use the keyboard shortcut instead: **Command Q.**

If you haven't saved all of your changes in any of the open documents when you choose to quit, the Mac will politely ask if you want to save them at this point (it also asks when you close an unsaved document). Thank goodness.

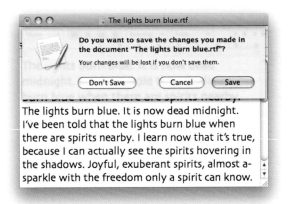

This is what each button in the above dialog box will do:

- Single-click the **Don't Save** button if you decide at this point you don't want the changes (or the entire document, *if* you've never named it).

    You can use the keyboard shortcut Command D instead of actually clicking the "Don't Save" button. In some applications, you can just hit the letter D.

- Single-click **Cancel** to return to your document without saving any changes or quitting. You can use the keyboard shortcut Command Period to cancel *instead* of clicking on the button.

- If you single-click **Save** and you haven't yet saved the document with a name, you'll get the "Save As..." dialog box (pages 84–85) to name the document before quitting.

    You can hit the Return or Enter key *instead* of clicking the Save button; in some applications you can hit the letter S.

The item "Quit" is always the last command in the application menu. If you don't see Quit in this menu, you are probably at the Desktop/Finder.

Quit when you are finished working in the application for the day. Once you quit, the application is removed from the computer's memory.

Alternatively, feel free to leave the application open for days on end, while you put your computer to sleep at night (see page 187). (If it starts acting a little funny or sluggish after a long while of staying open, quit and then open it back up again.)

Exercise 3: Quit TextEdit.

1 Make sure TextEdit is the active application: If you don't see "TextEdit" in your menu bar, as circled on page 107, single-click on its icon in the Dock.

2 From the File menu, choose "Quit." Or use the keyboard shortcut instead, Command Q.

Notice there is no longer a blue bubble under the TextEdit icon in the Dock.

There is a sweet little **shortcut to quit.** You don't even have to open the application to do this. Just *press* (don't click) on the application's icon in the Dock. In the pop-up menu that appears, choose "Quit."

Shortcut

Press on an open application icon to get this menu.

Sometimes an application acts so goofy that you have no choice but to **force quit.** For instance, you might see the spinning ball for much too long, or things just stop working in the application, or other weird stuff. And then when you try to quit, you can't!

Force Quit

If you have to force an application to quit, do one of these things:

- Press Command Option Escape (esc). A small dialog box appears; make sure the application name is chosen, then click the blue button to "Force Quit."

- Hold down the Option key and *press* (don't click) on the Dock icon. The command "Quit," as shown above, turns into "Force Quit."

You can't force quit the Finder, but you can "Relaunch" the Finder, which sometimes helps clean things up a bit if it starts "exhibiting puzzling behavior."

Quit applications upon Log Out, Restart, and Shut Down

When you choose to Log Out, Restart, or Shut Down (all from the Apple menu), the Mac will **automatically quit** all open applications for you (unless you have enabled "fast user switching" and are logging out so another user can log in; see *Mac OS X 10.5 Leopard: Peachpit Learning Series*).

If you have documents still open that have changes that need to be saved, you'll get a message for each one, giving you the opportunity to save it. This is a great option if you tend to leave lots of applications open—at the end of the day, instead of taking the time to quit each individual application, just Shut Down and they will all quit anyway.

This is the message you'll get if you choose to Log Out (from the Apple menu) while applications are still open. Click the "Log Out" button to start the process.

Note: If you have a lot of applications open, don't choose "Shut Down" or "Log Out" or "Restart" and then walk away from your computer! Wait until you see the blue screen because if there is an unsaved document anywhere on your Mac, a message will pop up asking you to save it. If you aren't there to deal with it, the Shut Down process (or Log Out or Restart) times out and your computer just sits there, patiently waiting for you to come back, which might be days.

To put something in the Trash, press-and-drag an icon over to the Trash can (actually, it looks like a wire wastebasket). When the basket turns dark, as shown below, let go and the file will drop inside. Don't let go of the file before the basket turns dark! If you find a bunch of garbage hanging around outside the Trash or sitting in the Dock, it's because you didn't wait for it to turn dark—you just set the trash down *next to* the basket.

The trick is that the **tip of the pointer** must touch the Trash basket! Whether you are putting one file in the Trash or whether you have selected several icons and are dragging them all together to the Trash, **the tip of the pointer** is what selects the wastebasket. The shadows of the objects have nothing to do with it—forget those shadows you see trailing along—just make sure the tip of the pointer touches the basket and highlights it (turns it dark). *Then* let go.

Anything you put in the Trash basket stays there, even if you turn off the computer, until you consciously empty the Trash (explained on the following page).

Trash a file

You can see the original file (the top one), plus the shadow that is pulled by the pointer (over the Trash basket). When the **tip of the pointer** touches the basket, the basket highlights, or turns dark. That means you can let go.

The paper in the basket is an obvious **visual clue** that there is something in the garbage.

Here you can see I selected three files. (I held down the Command key and clicked on each one.)

Then I **let go** of the Command key, dragged **one** of those selected files to the Trash, and the rest followed.

You can see all three shadows of the files, but notice where the pointer is. It's that **tip of the pointer, not** the shadows of the icons, that selects the Trash so the files can drop in.

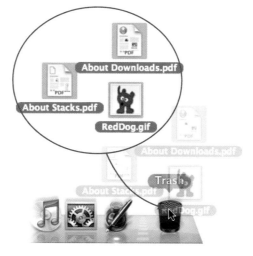

111

If you empty the Trash and tragically realize that you threw away your only copy of something very important, there is software and there are technicians who can often bring back your information. So if you lose something important, call your local guru, power user, or user group. In the meantime, don't turn off your computer or create new files.

In general, however, assume that when you toss something in the Trash, it's gone.

Exercise: Throw a file in the Trash basket.

1 If you did Exercise 2, you have a file in your Documents folder named "Toss This."

   Find that file so it's visible (single-click the Documents icon in the Sidebar, then scroll if necessary to find it).

2 Press (don't click) on that document icon and drag it to the Trash basket.

3 Make sure the tip of the pointer is positioned on the Trash basket, so the icon turns dark, then let go.

4 **To empty the Trash:** Press (don't click) on the Trash icon. A little menu pops up that says "Empty Trash." Select that item and let go.

More ways to trash files

There are several other ways to **move an item to the Trash** besides physically dragging a file and dropping it in the basket.

- Select the item (click once on it).
  From the File menu, choose "Move to Trash."

- *Or* select the item (click once on it).
  Press Command Delete.

- *Or* hold down the Control key (not the Command key) and single-click on a file you want to throw away. A con-textual menu pops up and gives you, among other things, the option to move that item to the Trash. Choose it.

Also Try This

To remove an item from the Trash *before* you have emptied it, single-click on the Trash icon. It opens up to a window, just like any other window! So if you decide you want that item you just threw away, you can go get it. But don't forget—you can only get items back from the Trash if you have not emptied the Trash!

Remove an item from the Trash

- If you change your mind directly after you throw something away, press Command Z (the "Undo" command) and the item you just put in the Trash will be instantly put back where it came from.

  Remember that Command Z acts as Undo for *the very last action you did;* that is, if you put a second file in the Trash, it is the second file that will be put back, not the first one. Or if you threw away a file and then you made a copy of a different file, Undo (Command Z) will undo the copying, not the trashing.

- You can always open the Trash window and drag the file out of the window and put it back where it belongs, as long as you have not emptied the Trash yet.

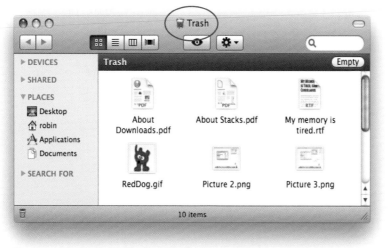

The Trash basket opens to a window. Drag any file out and put it wherever you want.

You might want to open another window (Command N) so you can move items from this Trash window to another window, or drag an item out of the window pane and drop it on one of the icons in your Sidebar, such as your Documents folder.

113

Remember

- The command to **Close** will close just that active window, it does not close the application.
- The command to **Quit** will quit the active application. If you have unsaved documents still open, you will be asked if you want to save them first. Thank goodness.
- Anything you put in the **Trash** will stay there, even if you turn off the computer or if the power goes out, until you choose to empty the trash.

Get Connected 9

If your Mac is already connected to the Internet, skip this entire chapter! If you just turned on your Mac and it's asking you strange questions about your Internet Service Provider or your connection method, read this chapter before you continue with the setup. **OR** skip the setup and come back to this chapter when you're **ready to make a connection.**

In this chapter

You need an Internet Service Provider

If you are already connected to the Internet, skip this entire chapter!

So how do you get to the Internet and the World Wide Web? You need a computer and a browser—one is your Mac, of course, and the browser (called Safari) is already on your Mac. Plus you need an Internet Service Provider. And you need a modem.

You see, you can't hook into the Internet directly from your own computer—you must go through an **Internet Service Provider (ISP).** From your home or business, you need to *pay* a provider to provide you with a connection to the Internet. You pay them; they connect you to the Internet; if you're using a phone modem, they'll give you a local phone number to dial in.

An Internet Service Provider will also give you one or more email addresses. (But not everyone who gives you an email address also provides an Internet connection! For instance, you can get a free email account at Gmail.com or yahoo.com, but neither Gmail.com nor yahoo.com is a *provider;* they cannot get you connected to the Internet.)

There are probably several Internet Service Providers in your area. There are also a couple of national providers that can set you up with a connection. Ask around your town and at your local Mac user group for the names of the favored providers.

Before you try to get connected, you must first establish a relationship with a provider! ("Establish a relationship" = pay them money.) The provider will give you the information necessary to continue with the setup process, as explained on the following pages. You can set up your connection at any time; that is, if you are ready when you first turn on your Mac to set it up, you can do that. Or you can skip the Internet setup at that time and do it next week or next month or next year, as explained on the following pages

Before you can get connected in the first place, you need a **modem,** which is a device that transforms the data sent between computers. The kind of modem you need depends on how you plan to connect to the Internet.

You have basically two choices. You'll connect through a **high-speed broadband modem;** your ISP will provide you with that modem. Or you will connect through a **dial-up phone modem;** this modem might be built into your Mac (all older Macs have built-in modems; newer Macs only have them if you requested it).

If you have a choice, go for the **broadband**—*it's always on, it's fast, and Mac OS X really prefers broadband because so many features on your Mac rely on getting information from the Internet.*

High-speed broadband "always-on" connection such as DSL, ISDN, cable, T1, T3, or satellite: You will still use a modem—but it's not a telephone modem, you don't use the telephone jack in your Mac, and the modem is not built in to your Mac. The company that provides you with the broadband service will provide you with the modem. You will connect to this modem with an **Ethernet** cable, which you'll plug into the Ethernet port on your Mac. The connectors (the things on the ends) on an Ethernet cable look very similar to a standard phone cable, but a little larger. The Ethernet port looks very similar to the telephone modem port, but a little larger.

When you're connected through a broadband modem, you will **not dial** any phone numbers to connect—you will just open your browser and you're on the web. **It's always on.** You just open your email application and get your email.

More than one computer can connect at the same time with one broadband connection.

Dial-up phone modem account: Look at the back or side of your computer—the phone jack is for your telephone modem. If you connect through a phone line, you have what's called a **dial-up account** because your modem will dial a phone number to connect to your Internet Service Provider. Only one computer at a time can connect through the same dial-up account.

> **Note:** If you want to use the **fax** software on your Mac, you must plug the telephone cable into the modem port and into a wall jack or telephone, even if you have a broadband connection. A fax will not go through the broadband connection—it must go through the phone line. Few Macs today have a phone port!

You need a modem

This is the Ethernet port on your Mac. DO NOT plug a phone line into this—it won't work!

You will use an Ethernet cable to connect your Mac to a broadband modem.

This is the phone modem port on your Mac. It looks just like a phone jack in your house. Compare it with the Ethernet port above.

117

Step by Step: What to do

Below are the **steps** you will need to follow to get yourself connected to the Internet so you can browse the World Wide Web and do email.

These are the basic steps to follow:

1 Choose an **Internet Service Provider,** call them up, and pay your money (see the previous pages).

2 Get your **modem** hooked up (if you're getting broadband, the ISP will get it hooked up for you; if you're using a dial-up modem, plug the phone cable into your Mac and into the phone jack in your wall).

3 Get the **setup information** from your provider. See the next two pages.

4 **Either** walk through the **setup process** if you're turning on your Mac for the first time, and fill in the information (pages 122–127 show screens similar to those you'll see during the initial setup.)

   Or do it yourself: During the initial setup process, click the button that says you'll connect later. After you get your Mac all put together, then use the Network preferences. (See pages 122–127.)

5 After you've set up the preferences, you're **ready to connect.**

   If you have a **broadband account,** just open your browser or email program; see page 124.

   If you have a telephone modem with a **dial-up account,** use Network system preferences; see pages 125–127.

6 Once you're online, see page 129 about how to **disconnect,** if necessary (it's not necessary to disconnect if you have a broadband account).

Whether you walk through the Setup Assistant the first time you turn on your Mac, *or* you decide to do it later, there is **information you need to have** from your Internet Service Provider (ISP) or network administrator. (If you use or plan to use America Online as your only connection, you don't need to go through this Internet setup process at all—installing AOL will do it for you!)

Have the information your provider gave you before you begin:

- User account name and password.
- Email address and password *(which might or might not be the same as your account name and password—sometimes it is not!).*
- If the account is broadband, ask your provider for the connection type and ask if you'll need a router number. In most cases, you probably won't need this, so if you can't get this information, carry on anyway!
- If you are on a local area network (LAN) in a large corporation or school, ask your system administrator for the pertinent information.
- If the account is a dial-up connection, you need the phone number, plus they might give you several DNS (domain name server) numbers that look something like this: **198.162.34.8.**

Write all of this information down! I guarantee you will need it again someday! And don't forget to write down every password as well.

I actually keep a small Rolodex file of account names and passwords for online accounts, email, catalogs, libraries, Apple, Adobe, eBay, airlines, bookstores, etc.

If you choose not to set up your email account in the inital setup process when you first get your Mac, you can always do it later. See Chapter 11.

To add an existing email account during the initial setup process, you will need:

- Your email address at that account.

- **Incoming mail server name.** This will be something like **mail.myDomainName.com** *or* **pop.myDomainName.com.**

  This is not always the same as your provider's name. For instance, I own the domain "ratz.com" and I get email there, so my *incoming mail server* name for that particular email account is "mail.ratz.com." But my *provider* is comcast.net.

- **Outgoing mail server (SMTP).** SMTP stands for Simple Mail Transfer Protocol, but who cares. This information will look something like **smtp.myProvider.com.**

  The SMTP is *always* the name of your Internet Service Provider because that is where your email gets sent *out* from. No matter how many different email accounts you have *coming in,* your *outgoing* mail server is always the one you are paying money to for your Internet connection; it is always your service provider.

  If you have a .Mac (dot Mac) email address, your SMTP is still the name of the ISP you **pay** for your Internet connection, *not* mac.com or Apple.

  Well, technically, that's not quite true! You actually *can* use a different SMTP, such as mac.com, but I guarantee you will have fewer problems if you use your provider's SMTP for every account. When you know you need a different SMTP, perhaps for traveling or other purposes, call your provider and ask what your options are for outgoing mail while you are away from your home/office connection.

- **Account type: IMAP or POP.** Most email accounts are POP accounts. Services like America Online and .Mac are IMAP accounts. Ask your provider to be sure; if you can't get hold of them, choose POP for now and you can always change it later once you find out.

POP: Post Office Protocol

IMAP: Internet Message Access Protocol

You can get connected to the Internet during the setup process the first time you turn on your new Mac, or you can do it at any time after your computer is up and running. The questions are the same either way. Apple has made it so easy to connect to the Internet that you could be surfing the web in just a few clicks.

Before you start the process, make sure your modem is plugged into the wall appropriately (depending on what kind of modem you have), that there is a cable connecting the modem to your Mac, and that everything is turned on.

In the process of getting connected to the Internet, the Mac will ask if you want a **.Mac account** (pronounced *dot mac*) which costs $99 a year. You'll get an email account at Mac.com (although you still need an Internet Service Provider), storage space on Apple's server so you can share files across the Internet, and much more. To learn about a .Mac account:

- **Either** single-click the ".Mac" button that appears in the setup screen to get a little tour from Apple.

- **Or** click "No" for now. After your connection is setup, go to **www.mac.com** and see if it's something you want.

- **Or** after you are connected to the Internet, open your System Preferences (see page 122), click the ".Mac" icon, then click the "Learn More" button. This will take you to the Mac.com site.

If you're turning on your Mac for the first time, it will ask you similar questions to the ones you see following this page. **If you computer is already running,** you'll use the Network preferences as explained on the following pages.

You will also need to use these Network preferences when you decide to switch providers, when you upgrade to a broadband connection from a dial-up, when you connect your Macs over Ethernet to share files, when things go wrong, etc.

Getting ready to set up

What's a .Mac account?

If you already have a .Mac account, your Mac will set it up for you automatically as soon as you enter your user name and password.

Use Network preferences

Network

AOL users: When you install AOL, its Setup Assistant will walk you through the process to get your email directly in the Mail application that's in your Dock.

121

Set up your broadband connection

As I mentioned on the previous page, the questions are the same whether you are installing a new operating system on your Mac, turning your Mac on for the first time right out of the box, or setting up the connection long after you've been using the computer. The windows look a little different, but the information is the same.

To open and use the Network preferences:

1 From the Apple menu, choose "System Preferences…," *or* click on the System Preferences icon in the Dock.

2 Single-click on the "Network" icon. The network status of your current connection is displayed in the left-hand pane of this window, as shown below. You may see more than one "service" possibility in this list.

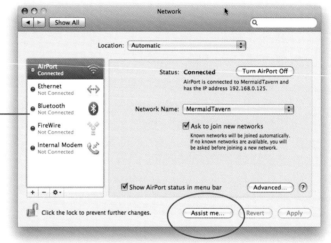

Your Mac compiles this list depending on your computer and what kinds of cables and hardware (like modems) you have attached.

3 **To let your Mac guide you** through the setup process, click the "Assist me…" button, shown circled above. A little sheet drops down, shown below: Click "Assistant…."

You will be guided through a series of simple screens in which you'll choose or enter information, as shown on the next page.

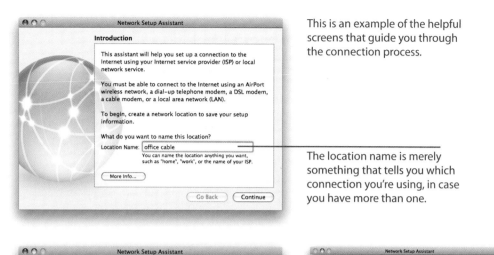

This is an example of the helpful screens that guide you through the connection process.

The location name is merely something that tells you which connection you're using, in case you have more than one.

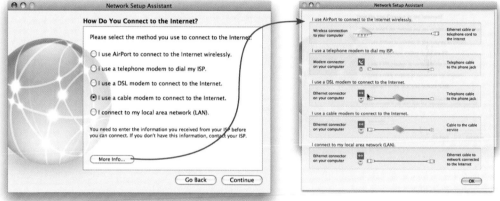

If you're not sure about what kind of connection you have, click the "More Info…" button for a description of the possible services.

If you are in an office that is connected to the Internet through an ISDN, T1, or T3 line, your Mac is not **directly** connected to an incoming modem box, so you will choose "local area network (LAN)."

With a cable connection, DSL, or a LAN, that's all you need to do!

The **AirPort wireless** connection needs to know your password, if there is one, and assumes that someone has previously set up your AirPort.

Connect to the Internet with your broadband account

If you have a **broadband account,** then you are already connected to the Internet. All you have to do is open a browser or your email application and there you are. It's fabulous.

You don't need to disconnect—broadband is an "always on" connection.

Some low-class broadband providers will make you go through a little connection process, like a dial-up, which defeats half the purpose of having a broadband connection. Try to find a company that doesn't do that.

Set the service order

Here is an important **troubleshooting tip.** If you have more than one way to connect to the Internet, your Mac follows a certain order in trying to establish a connection. If you're having trouble, you can change this order so the computer first tries to connect with your preferred service.

To change the connectivity order of services:

1　In the Network system preferences, single-click on the Action menu, shown circled below. From the menu that pops up, choose "Set Service Order...."

2　The sheet you see below drops down from the toolbar. All the services are listed. *Press on the one you use to connect and drag it to the very top.* Click OK.

Drag your preferred service to the top of the list. Watch the dark line—when you let go, the service will land where the dark line is.

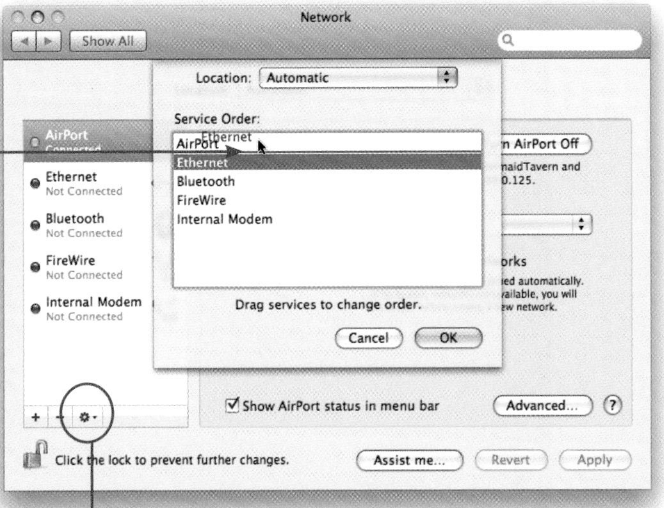

This is the Action menu.

Follow Steps 1–3 on page 122. After the first screen where you name the location, you'll see these windows:

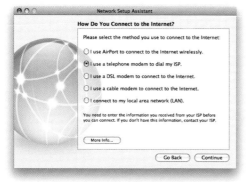

Choose the telephone modem option.

Enter your account name and password, *which might be different* from your email account name and password! Check with your ISP.

Enter the phone number they gave you. This is not your phone number—it is the phone number your modem will dial to connect to the Internet.

Your Mac has checked to see which modem is installed and connected.

That's it! See the following pages for a couple of extra settings you might like to change.

125

Extra options for phone modem connections

If you have a dial-up connection through your phone line, you can enter the information directly into the Network preferences, as explained on the previous page.

Remember, the account name and password, in this pane, is your account name and password *with your service provider.* Sometimes these are different from your email name and password! You can change your email password whenever you like, but your account password for your ISP is given to you by your provider and cannot be changed unless you call them up and arrange it.

To check the other settings for your dial-up account, click the "Advanced…" button in the Network preferences, shown below.

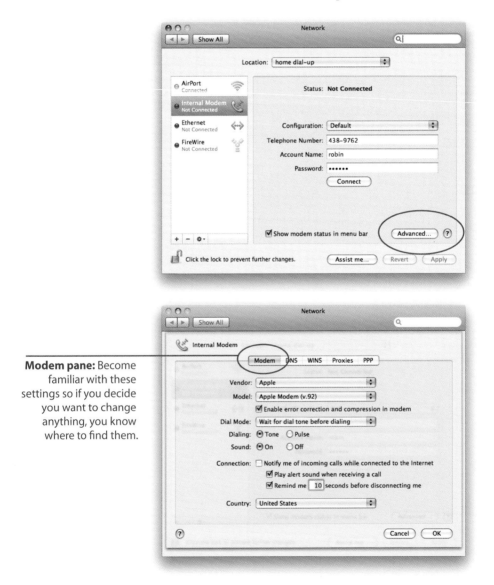

Modem pane: Become familiar with these settings so if you decide you want to change anything, you know where to find them.

PPP pane: Because your Mac goes to the Internet so often, for everything from help files to updates for software, you might like to make sure the box is checked to "Connect automatically when needed." However, if your Mac shares your regular phone line, you might *not* want this checked so your Mac won't try to connect while you need the phone.

If you keep getting disconnected when you're not expecting it, one thing that might help is to uncheck the box "Disconnect if idle for 10 minutes," or at least enter a number larger than 10. (Your dial-up service provider will probably disconnect you after a certain length of idle time.)

Decide for yourself how you want the other options set.

Connect to the Internet with a dial-up account

Okay, you're all set up with your new telephone modem **Internet** account and you want to actually **connect** and go to the web. There are several ways to do this.

Connect automatically

If you checked the box, **"Connect automatically when needed,"** as explained on the previous page, then you can just single-click on the Mail icon or the Safari browser icon in your Dock. The Mac will automatically dial up your connection and log on, then open the application.

If you have any trouble doing that, manually log on to the Internet yourself, as explained below, and *then* open your browser.

Use the modem status icon

If you have the modem status icon in your menu bar, go to it and choose "Connect Internal Modem." You'll hear the modem start squeaking and the icon in the menu bar will send off "sound waves" to indicate that you are connecting and connected.

If the modem icon is not in your menu bar, you can add it; see the opposite page.

Once you are connected to the Internet, open your browser or email application and surf or check your mail.

If you choose "Open Network Preferences...," you'll get the dialog box shown on the opposite page.

If you do not have the modem status icon in your menu bar, open the Network system preferences again, as explained on page 122.

Click the **Connect** button to connect to the Internet. Then open your browser or email application and surf or check your mail.

Use the Network preferences to connect

Network

Check this box if you want the modem status icon to appear in your menu bar.

To disconnect your phone from the Internet, click the "Disconnect" command from the modem menu.

Once you are connected, the "Connect" button shown above in the Network system preferences changes to "Disconnect"—click it to disconnect from the Internet.

Disconnect your dial-up account

- If you have a **broadband** connection, you are *always* connected to the Internet (unless you use a crummy provider) and you can instantly open and use your browser or email program anytime you like, night or day.

- If you have a **dial-up** account, your provider will disconnect you if you are "idle" (not actively using the connection) for a certain length of time (a time that they determine; you might want to ask what that is).

Are ya ratty for the Net?

Surf the Web

Different things you do on your Macintosh require different applications. To browse the web, you'll use the software application called a **browser.** In your Dock, you have an icon for the browser called Safari.

This is the Safari icon that you should see in the Dock. If it's not there, you'll find it in your Applications folder.

You can view web pages in your browser, watch movies, hear music, print from your browser, and on and on. In this chapter I'm going to give you some basic tips that will get you started right away.

I don't capitalize "web" since we don't capitalize other forms of communication such as radio, television, or telephone.

In this chapter

What are web pages?

The World Wide Web is comprised of several billion individual **web pages.** These pages are quite the same as the pages you create in your word processor—in fact, many of them are created in word processors, and the code for most web pages can be viewed in a word processor.

The big deal about web pages is that they have "hypertext links"— text you click on to make another page appear in front of you. It's like this: Imagine that you could open a book to its table of contents and touch, say, "Chapter 3," and the book instantly flips to Chapter 3. In Chapter 3, there is a reference to Greek mythology. You touch the word "Greek mythology," and a book about Greek mythology instantly appears in front of you, open to the page you want. As you're reading about Greek mythology, you see a reference to goddess worship so you touch that reference and instantly that book appears in front of you, open to the page you want. That's what web pages do, that's what hypertext is. That's what's incredible.

What is a web address?

Even though there are several billion web pages on the Internet right now, every web page has its own **address,** just like every house in the country has an address of some sort. The address is sometimes called a **URL** (pronounced *you are ell*). When you get to page 137, you'll learn exactly how to enter a URL.

If you want to connect right now

You don't have to **connect to the Internet** and the web to read this chapter—you can skim through and get the gist of how to use your browser and the web.

But if you have a **full-time broadband connection** (something like a cable modem, DSL, ISDN, or T1 line) and want to connect so you can experiment in this chapter, all you need to do to get to the Internet is single-click the Safari browser icon in your Dock.

This is the icon for the browser that came with your Mac, called Safari. If you have a full-time (broadband) connection, just single-click this icon to get to the web.

If your connection uses a **telephone modem,** please see pages 125–129 for details about connecting.

If you're **not connected at all** or if you have no idea how you are connected, please see the previous chapter.

Every web page has **links** on it. Single-click a link with your mouse and a new web page appears. A link might be text or it might be a graphic. If it's text, it often has an underline, or at least it's in a different color; if it's a graphic, it sometimes has a border around it. Even if the **visual clues** of the underline or the border are missing, you can always tell when something is a link because the pointer turns into a hand with a pointing finger, as shown to the right. Just run your mouse over the page *(without pressing the button down)* and you'll see the pointer turn into the browser hand whenever you "mouse over" a link.

What are links?

This is a typical "browser hand" that you'll see in a browser.

This is a typical web page. You can see the browser hand positioned over colored text, about to click the link to go to "The Product" page.

Not all links have underlines; the browser hand tells you what is a link.

When you click on a link like the one circled above, "The Product," the browser jumps to another page, in this case the page shown to the right. You can see there are more links on this new page. You can click links for the rest of your life and still not have time to read everything.

That's the World Wide Web.

Exercise 1: Poke around some web pages.

1 Apple has set a default (an automatic action) for Safari that takes you to a particular web page (usually an Apple page) when you open Safari for the first time. That web page has lots of links. Just single-click any link on that page that interests you. Poke around for a while!

2 To go to pages you have previously visited, use the Back and Forward buttons, as shown on the opposite page.

3 To go to a particular page whose web address you know, see page 137 (try going to www.UrlsInternetCafe.com).

You see **buttons** in your **toolbar.** The ones you will use most often are "Back" and "Forward." The Back button, of course, takes you back through pages you have visited. Once you've gone back, then the Forward button appears so you can go forward again.

Go back and forth from page to page

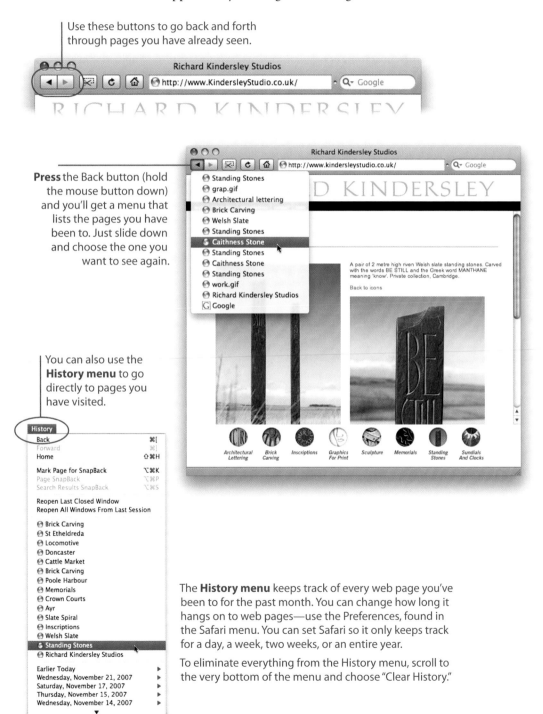

Use these buttons to go back and forth through pages you have already seen.

Press the Back button (hold the mouse button down) and you'll get a menu that lists the pages you have been to. Just slide down and choose the one you want to see again.

You can also use the **History menu** to go directly to pages you have visited.

The **History menu** keeps track of every web page you've been to for the past month. You can change how long it hangs on to web pages—use the Preferences, found in the Safari menu. You can set Safari so it only keeps track for a day, a week, two weeks, or an entire year.

To eliminate everything from the History menu, scroll to the very bottom of the menu and choose "Clear History."

**Open a new
browser window**

You can have lots and **lots of browser windows open.** This comes in handy when you really like a page, or maybe a page has lots of interesting links you want to follow and when you go to another page you don't want this one to disappear. So instead of clicking on the link to get another page, Control-click on it (hold the Control key down and click once). You will get a menu right there in the middle of the page, and one of the options is "Open Link in New Window." Choose that option—a new window with the new page will open *in front of* the previous window.

The Back button on the new page will be gray because, since this is a new window, it has no where to go back to! Your original page still retains all of the Back pages.

Hold down the Control key and click on a link to get a menu like this. If you have a two-button mouse, ignore the Control key and use the right button instead.

Discussions	
Discussion Lead	**Open Link in New Window**
Previous Discus	Open Link in New Tab
King Lear Discus	Download Linked File
What Others Say	Download Linked File As...
Contact	Add Link to Bookmarks...
	Copy Link

Discussions run twelve to

Exercise 2: Try these other two tips for opening windows.

1 Open a page in a new window: Command-click on a link. The new page opens *on top of* the existing page. Just move it out of the way if you want to see the original window.

2 Open a page in a new window, but make that window *go behind* the current window: Command Shift-click on a link.

Check the Dock

When multiple web pages are open, they will all be displayed in the **Dock pop-up menu.** Just *press* (don't click) on the Safari icon in the Dock, as shown below, and choose the page you want to come forward.

Press on the Safari
icon in the Dock.

To enter a web address, type it into the "Location" box at the **top** of the window, in the toolbar. **After you type it in,** hit Return or Enter to tell the browser to go find that page. Notice carefully in the illustrations below where the Location box is located!

Enter a web address

This is where you type the web address (the URL).

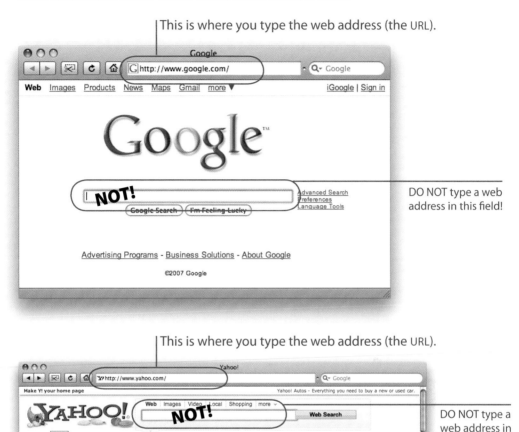

DO NOT type a web address in this field!

This is where you type the web address (the URL).

DO NOT type a web address in this field!

Exercise 3: **Enter a web address.**

1 Select the text that is currently in the Location box (an easy way to do that is to press Command L).

2 Type a web address, such as **www.mac.com** (you don't have to type **http://**).

3 Hit the Return or the Enter key to go to the site. Voilà!

Shortcut to enter address

And here's an extra-special **shortcut** you will love. On the Mac, you don't have to type in the entire ugly web address with the http:// and all. For one thing, you never need to type http://. So skip that part altogether. If the rest of the address is in this format, www.**something**.*com,* all you need to type is **something**. Really.

For instance, to go to http://www.**apple**.com, all you need to type is **apple**, then hit Return or Enter. The browser looks for a *.com* address with the name you entered, and if it finds one, it takes you there. (If the browser cannot find a web site with that "domain" name, it does a search for that topic and shows you the results of the search.)

If the address uses another domain identifier, such as *.org* or *.net* instead of *.com,* you'll have to type *.org* or *.net,* etc. And if the address has other slashes and stuff, you'll have to type everything after the domain (the domain is the <u>company.com</u> part).

Exercise 4: Use a web address shortcut.

1 In Safari, type Command L. This will highlight the Location box where you enter an address.

2 Type **apple**

3 Hit Return.

4 Try it with other names of companies who surely have their own web sites, such as Sears, NFL, Disney, etc. (And remember, you don't have to type capital letters until after the end of the domain. But *after* the domain slash, it is absolutely critical that you type a capital letter or lowercase letter exactly as shown.)

http://www.TheUnderstanders.com/

You don't ever have to type this part.

In this area, it doesn't matter whether you type capitals or lowercase.

After this slash, you MUST type capitals or lowercase as the web address is written.

You can **choose your own Home page.** "Home," in a browser, is the page you find yourself going to the most while you're surfing the web. For instance, I chose **Google.com** as my home page. John likes **News.Google.com** for instant access to news.

When you click the "Home" icon in the toolbar, Safari instantly displays the web page you have chosen as your home page.

Choose your Home page

This is the **Home** button. If you don't see it, follow Step 6, below.

This is the **Bookmarks Bar;** see the next page.

Exercise 5: **Choose your Home page.**

1. Single-click on a blank area of a web page to make sure Safari is active.

2. From the Safari menu, choose "Preferences...."

3. Single-click the "General" icon in the toolbar.

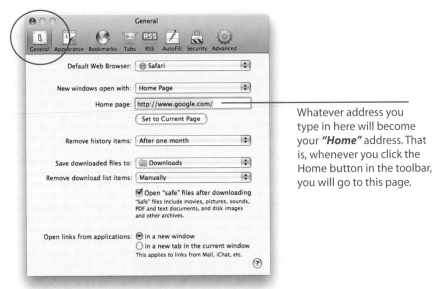

Whatever address you type in here will become your **"Home"** address. That is, whenever you click the Home button in the toolbar, you will go to this page.

4. In the "Home page" field, type the complete web address of the page you want as your Home page.

5. Click the red Close button.

6. If you don't have a Home button in your Safari toolbar, put it there: From the View menu, choose "Customize Address Bar...." Drag the Home icon into the toolbar. Click the "Done" button.

7. Single-click that Home button in the toolbar and it takes you to the web page you specified.

139

Bookmarks

As you wander around the web, you'll run across web sites you really like and want to come back to. For these sites, make a **Bookmark:** simply press Command D while viewing the page. You'll be asked to give the bookmark a name that means something to you. Once you have a bookmark, that page shows up in your Bookmarks menu and you can just choose it from that menu.

This is a bookmarks list. Whenever I want to return to one of these pages, I choose it from the Bookmarks menu.

As you make lots of bookmarks, you'll need to organize them. Safari has fabulous tools for organizing your bookmarks, but this book is getting too big already—please see *Cool Mac Apps* for all the amazing details about bookmarks in Safari, as well as everything else you need to know about using this great browser.

Exercise 6: Make and use a bookmark.

1 Go to any page that you want to be able to find again quickly.

2 While viewing that page, press Command D, *or* go to the Bookmarks menu and choose "Add Bookmark."

3 A little sheet drops down and asks you to name the bookmark: The name of the web page is already *selected (highlighted),* so just type to change the name.

It also asks you where to save it: From the little pop-up menu on that sheet, choose "Bookmarks Menu." *

*If you want instant access to favorite sites, choose to save the bookmark in the **"Bookmarks Bar."** The link will be put into that little bar above the web page, as shown on the previous page.

4 Now go to a few other web pages, just clicking on random links.

5 **To go to your bookmarked page,** single-click on the Bookmarks menu, then slide down and choose the bookmark that you added just a minute ago.

Exercise: You can put a link to a web page right in your Dock.

1 In Safari, go to the page you want to put in the Dock.

2 See that tiny icon to the left of the web address in the location box? Drag that tiny icon down to the *right* side of the dividing line in the Dock, then let go.

3 You'll get one of those springy-things in the Dock. Whenever you want to go to that page, just single-click the spring. If your browser is not open, this will open it.

Put a web page link in your Dock

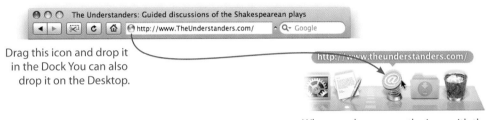

Drag this icon and drop it in the Dock You can also drop it on the Desktop.

When you hover over the icon with the mouse, you'll see the web page name.

Search tools

Once you know how to use your browser and start surfing, you'll quickly run up against this problem: There are several billion web pages out there. How do you find the one you want? You find it with a **search tool,** often referred to as a search engine. You don't have to buy or install search tools—they are just on the web, like any of the other web pages. But they are different from other web pages in that you can type in the names of subjects you want to find, and the search tool will look for it.

Oh, there is so much to tell you about search tools, but that's not the purpose of this book. I can only tell you a couple of important points, and you will have to move on from there.

When you enter a query in a search tool, it does not go running all over the world looking for pages that match your query. **It looks only in its own database** that it has compiled according to its own special criteria. There are many search tools, and they each have their own criteria and their own way of adding sites to their database. So you might ask three different search tools to find "Briards" and come up with three very different lists of web pages about Briards (a dog breed).

Important Point Number One

Every search tool has different rules for finding information. **Read the Tips or Help section.** It will tell you critical details about how to enter a query so results can be found. As search tools are improved, their rules change, so when you see a new look on your favorite search page, check the Help section again.

Important Point Number Two

Search using Google

Enter this web address: **google.com.**

Or, no matter which page you're viewing, you can use this field to search in Google!

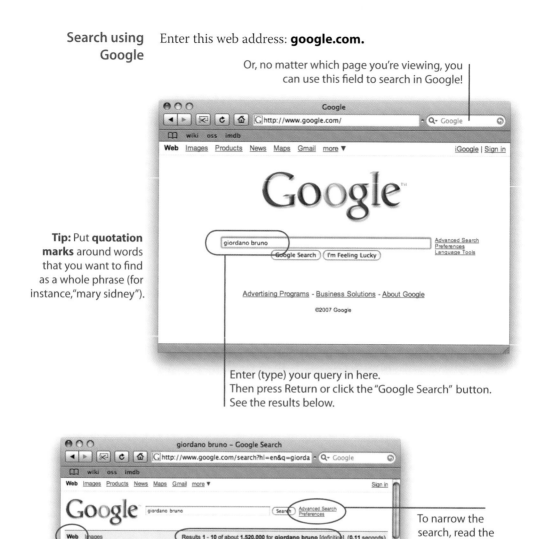

Tip: Put **quotation marks** around words that you want to find as a whole phrase (for instance, "mary sidney").

Enter (type) your query in here.
Then press Return or click the "Google Search" button.
See the results below.

To narrow the search, read the search tips page of the web site! Every search tool gives you tips on how to find specifically the item you want.

These are the results of the simple search shown above.
Single-click any link to go to that page.

If you Command-click on a link, the new page will open in a **new window.** That way you won't lose this page full of results.

Or after you go to another page, click on the **tiny orange arrow** that appears in the Google field (see above, top-right corner) to return to this page of results.

Find a search tool you like and then spend some time getting to know all of its features. In this example, I clicked the link to search for "Images," typed "solpugid," and got the results shown below.

Tip: In Google, put a – sign (minus sign or hyphen) in front of a word to exclude that word.

For instance, to search for images of the bird **phoenix,** but not the city, enter:

  phoenix bird –arizona

To make sure pages about River Phoenix the actor don't appear either, enter:

  phoenix bird –arizona –river

Explore the rest of Google

Google is an incredible tool. Click the "more" link, as shown below, to see some of the other tools Google has created or is in the process of creating. Each of the links across the top and in the menu indicates another specialized service. Use **Maps** to get visual and written directions to anywhere in the United States, and to see a satellite image of places around the world. Use **Groups** to locate discussions and support groups devoted to specific topics and concerns. Use **Products** to comparitively shop for millions of items from hundreds of stores. And so much more! Amazing.

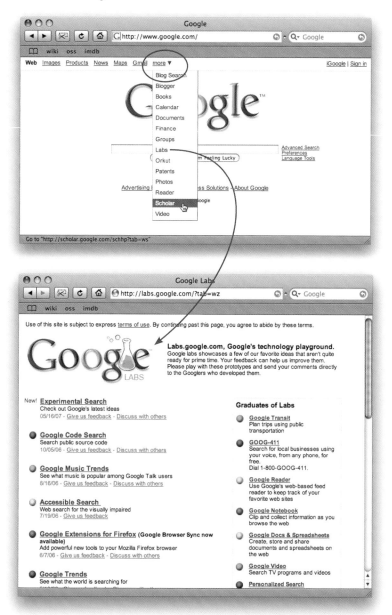

Here are a few **web addresses** you might find handy. Web addresses have a habit of changing as soon as you print them in a book, so I've tried to give you only well-established sites that might not change soon. If they have changed and any of these addresses don't work, I apologize!

URLs for you

Macintosh	MacinTouch.com, MacWorld.com/news, MacMinute.com, MacFixIt.com, TidBits.com, MacOSXhints.com, MacObserver.com, MacInsider.com, Apple.com
Books (retail)	Amazon.com, BN.com *(Barnes & Noble)*
For writers	Bookwire.com *(inside the book world)*
Family	Family.com
Movies	Fandango.com, IMDB.com *(Internet Movie Database)*
Quotations	QuotationsPage.com, Quoteland.com, CreativeQuotations.com
Sports	ESPN.com, SportsIllustrated.com
Travel	LonelyPlanet.com, Travel.Discovery.com
Weather	AccuWeather.com, Weather.com
Music	Listen.com, RollingStone.com, AllMusic.com
Science	Discovery.com, SciAm.com *(Scientific American)*
Games	GamesMania.com
Health	ReutersHealth.com, Health.com, VH.org *(The Virtual Hospital)*
Money	Money.cnn.com
Genealogy	Genealogy.com, Ancestry.com, GenHomePage.com
Recipes	AllRecipes.com, Epicurious.com
Stain removal	Tide.com
Gardening	Gardening.com, OrganicGardening.com, KidsGardening.com
Home improvements, recipes, decorating	BHG.com *(Better Homes & Gardens)*
IRS	IRS.gov *(download IRS forms)*
Peachpit Press	Peachpit.com

Also go to **About.com** and search for whatever you're interested in.

As indicated above, you don't need to type "www" on any of these particular addresses.

- You don't need to type **http://** in a web address.
- Make and use your **bookmarks!**
- Read the **search tips** in Google to learn how to find what you want on the web.
- Take advantage of the **Home** button!

The Mac application for email is called **Mail.** As you'd expect, with Mail you can write email messages, send messages, and receive messages—that's what this chapter covers. Mail actually goes way beyond those basic functions; it has many useful tools for organizing, formatting, searching, and filtering email. But to keep this book "little," I had to put the more detailed information about the other features into *Cool Mac Apps, third edition.* This chapter in your hands, however, will get you sending and receiving email and attachments, using Notes and To Dos, and creating fancy stationery.

You must have an Internet connection already set up, as explained in Chapter 9, and you must **already have an email account** with someone.

The **Address Book** is a separate application that works in conjunction with Mail. You can save your favorite email addresses, make a group list to send a message to a number of people at once, enter an address in a new message with the click of the mouse, and more.

In this chapter

Set up your account

Before Mail can check your email account, you must **set up your account.** *If you entered your email information when you first turned on your Mac, Mail is ready to go and you can skip to page 150.* If not, you need the information listed below to create an account. This information comes from your Internet Service Provider (ISP), as explained in Chapter 9, so if you don't know what an ISP is, please read that information!

Email address: Your provider gave you an email address, or asked you to create one. It looks something like this:

yourname@isp.com   *or*   yourname@earthlink.net

Incoming mail server: Your provider will tell you exactly what this is. It's usually something like this:

mail.mac.com   *or*   pop.earthlink.net

> *Advanced note:* If you have an ISP but you also have several different email accounts from other places, such as from your own domain or someone's web site, ask your host for that account what the incoming mail server is.

Account type: It's usually either a POP account or IMAP. A .Mac account is IMAP; most local providers are POP.

User name: This is *usually* the same as your email address, but *not always* because it's actually the user name for your account *with that provider.* Use your email address as your user name, and if it doesn't work, call your provider and ask them what it is.

Password: This should be the password for your email, but if that won't work, call your provider and ask if they have a different password for your *Internet account* than they have for your *email account.*

Outgoing Mail Server, or SMTP: No matter how many email accounts you have from how many different places, this is always the name of the provider you pay each month to connect you to the Internet. For instance, I have a dozen different email accounts at a dozen different servers, but the SMTP for every one of them is the same—it is Comcast because that's who I pay each month. That's who all of my email goes out through. An SMTP address usually looks something like this:

smtp.comcast.net

When you open Mail for the first time, it will ask you for the information as shown below and explained on the opposite page. If you already set up your Mail account when you first turned on your Mac, you can skip to page 150.

Enter your existing email account name and password.

For information about your "incoming mail server," see the opposite page.

There are just a couple of windows like this where you will be asked to fill in the information.

Don't worry if you don't know exactly what to enter here—you can always change it, as shown below, or click "Cancel" and fill in the account information later.

You can add more accounts, change existing information, and customize your accounts from the Mail preferences dialog box: Go to the Mail menu, choose "Preferences…," and single-click the Accounts button in the toolbar.

To add another account, single-click the **+** sign.

If you type your email password in here, you won't have to enter it every time you check your mail. This means, however, that anyone on your computer can check your email.

Mail

The **basic** things you will be doing in **Mail** are checking messages, replying to messages, and composing new messages. On these next few pages are directions for how to do just that. But don't neglect Notes and To Do items!

The Viewer window

Mail opens up to the **Viewer window.** If you open Mail and don't see this window, press Command Option N (or go to the File menu and choose "New Viewer Window").

This is the Message List.

Blue dot:	You have not yet read that message.
Green dot:	That person is one of your Buddies in iChat and is online at the moment.
Curved arrow:	You have sent a response.
Straight arrow:	You have forwarded this message.

Mailboxes sidebar. The number in parentheses indicates unread messages.

Inbox — orobin@mac.com (60 messages, 1 unread)

Get Mail   Delete   Junk   Reply   Reply All   Forward   New Message   Note   To Do   Search

MAILBOXES
▼ 📥 Inbox
  📧 orobin@mac.com (1)
  📄 TheShakespearePapers (8)
  📄 ratz (2)
▶ 📄 Drafts (2)
  ✉ Sent
▶ 🗑 Trash
  📥 Junk (1)

▶ RSS (42)

▶ OROBIN@MAC.COM

•	•	From	Subject	Date ▼	🖉
●	○	Pat Williams	stationery	Yesterday	🖉 7
↰		Denise Kusel	Hi Robin	Yesterday	
→		Neil R. Bauman	Shakespeare at Sea follow up	Yesterday	
		NarrativeMagazine.com	New at Narrative	11/20/07	
↰	○	Pat Williams	Re: Mom, I'm introducing you to Chuck	11/19/07	
↰		David Van Ness	Re: page count?	11/19/07	
↰		David Van Ness	FTP site for The Little Mac Book, Leopa...	11/19/07	
		zoom	Re: checking in	11/17/07	
↰		dearjimprice@mac.com	Home, safe and sound!	11/15/07	

From: Denise Kusel <kusel@mac.com>
Subject: **Hi Robin**
Date: November 24, 2007 6:23:23 PM GMT-04:00
To: Robin Williams <orobin@mac.com>

Just got back from Vermont and studying writing. Nothing to do but write. Leslie and I are thinking about getting Leopard -- the family pack since there are two of us -- wouldn't mind finding a few more folks to make up our family, but that isn't here nor there. The question is that Is Leopard worth it?
Is it as great as they say?
thanks a lot
Denise

ps
I wrote a novella and three short stories --- got a lot of work done!

Resize the Mailboxes sidebar.

Preview message pane. Single-click a message in the list above to preview it here; **double-click a message to open it in a separate window.**

Resize the Preview pane. **To get rid of this preview** so you don't have to look at junk mail before you delete it, drag this bar all the way to the bottom.

Resize the entire window.

If you don't know anyone's email address to write to, you can **write a message** to yourself, send it, and you'll get it within a few minutes.

Write and send an email message

Exercise 1: Write an email message and send it.

1 Click the "New Message" button in the toolbar to open a "New Message" window, as shown below (except yours will be blank).

New Message

An email address must have an @ symbol (at), and there must be a "domain name" with a dot, such as "ratz.com," "aol.com," "earthlink.net," etc.

2 Click in the "To" field and type an email address, as shown above. You can type more than one address in here, as long you type a comma after each one.

> **Note:** If the person you are sending email to is already in your Address Book or "Previous Recipients" list, Mail replaces the email address with that person's name as soon as you type it. If you need to change or edit that name, single-click on the name and a little menu pops up; choose the action you want to take (as shown below).

Don't be alarmed if the email address suddenly changes to a person's name. If you need to make any corrections, single-click on the name and you'll get the menu shown here.

—continued

3 If you want to send a copy of this same letter to someone else, click in the "Cc" field and type an address. You
can type more than one address, separated by a comma
and space.

Adding a name to the "Cc" field is really no different
from typing more than one address in the "To" field;
it's just a subtle understatement that the message really
belongs to the person in the "To" field, and someone
else is getting a copy of it for some reason.

4 Click in the "Subject" field and type a message description. *This is important*—the recipient needs to know
that your message is not junk mail.

5 Click in the blank message area and type your message!

6 Connect to the Internet if you're using a dial-up
account; if you have broadband, skip this step becuse
you're already connected.

7 Click the "Send" icon in the toolbar. Off it goes.

Your copy of the sent message will be stored in the Mail
sidebar in the "Sent" folder.

That was easy!

If you have a broadband Internet connection that is always on, you don't even have to open Mail to know if you have messages: The Mail icon in the Dock will tell you how many new messages you have.

When new messages arrive, the Mail icon in the Dock displays how many new messages you have.

If you have a dial-up connection, the number in the Dock only appears when you are connected and Mail has checked your account for new messages.

Exercise 2: Check for messages.

1 Connect to the Internet if you're not already connected.

2 Click once on the Mail icon in the Dock to open Mail.

3 Click the "Get Mail" icon in the toolbar.

Next to the Inbox (and in the Dock) you might see a number in bold—if you do, that number indicates how many *unread* messages are in your Inbox.

4 Single-click your Inbox. Your messages will appear in the Message List.

5 Single-click a message to display its contents in the Preview message pane.

If you deleted the message pane because you don't want to preview messages (see page 150), then double-click the message and it will open in its own window.

Exercise 3: Reply to the sender of a message.

1 If the message is not already open, double-click it in the Viewer window.

2 Single-click the "Reply" button in the toolbar.

3 A message window opens that contains the original sender's address in the "To" field, and the original message formatted as a quote (in color and with a line down the left side). Type your reply *above* the quote, then click the "Send" button in the toolbar.

> ***Tip:*** If you select a portion of the text *before* you click "Reply," just that portion of text will be copied into the new email message!

153

Tips for replying to messages

Here are a few extra tips to keep in mind as you reply to messages that have been sent to you.

To reply to *all* recipients of a message:

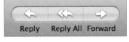

Mail that you receive may have been sent to multiple recipients either directly or as carbon copies (Cc). You can choose to reply to *all* recipients with one email (the reply will not include anyone in the hidden Bcc list; see the next page).

1 If the message is not already open, double-click the message in the Viewer window to open it.

2 In the message window, click the "Reply All" button in the toolbar.

3 Type your reply above the original quoted message, then click the "Send" button in the toolbar.

To forward a message:

A message that you forward is left in your box and a copy is sent to the person of your choice.

1 Double-click a message in the Viewer window.

2 Select the part of the message that you want to forward: press-and-drag over the specific text. Just the information you select will be forwarded. (If you really want to send the entire message, don't select anything before you go to Step 3.)

3 Click the "Forward" button in the toolbar.

Delete any and everything that is not part of the actual message; delete every email address from the message area!!! Do NOT forward a message full of garbage. Very bad things will happen if you forward meaningless junk.

4 Type your comments *above* the original quoted message, then click the "Send" button in the toolbar. It's really nice to add a personal message to anything you forward. And please don't forward stupid stuff—make sure it's worth someone's time to get it and that it's not loaded with a foot of garbage!

Here are a few extra tips to keep in mind as you compose new messages.

To save a message as a draft: If you need to finish a message later, click "Save As Draft" in the toolbar, *or* press Command S. The message will be saved in the Drafts folder within your Mailboxes sidebar. You will only see this button when you're writing a new message.

> Mail **automatically** creates a draft for you whenever you're writing a lengthy letter—in case something happens and your computer goes down, you won't lose the entire letter. But to make sure, press Command S regularly, as you would in any document.

To open the draft ("restore" it) later for editing, single-click the "Drafts" icon in the Mailboxes sidebar, then double-click the desired draft in the list. It will open and you can continue working on it.

To address a message using the Address Pane: Click the "Address" button in the New Message toolbar. This opens a *limited* version of your Address Book, called the Address Pane. You can't add names to this pane, but you can use it to automatically address your email message: Double-click a name in your list to address your message to that person.

> **To send the same message to more than one person,** hold down the Command key and single-click on any number of names in the Address Pane, then click the "To" button (or just double-click on each person's name and they will be added one at a time).

You'll only see this "Address" button when you're writing a new message, unless you customize the toolbar (use the View menu).

To send a Bcc (blind courtesy copy):

1. Address and write your message as usual.

2. From the little menu shown to the right, choose "Bcc Address Field." This puts a new field in the address area. Any address(es) you type in this field will *not* be seen by anyone whose address is in the "To" or "Cc" field.

Attach a file Sometimes you want to **send someone a photo** you took or a text file that you created in your word processor. You can send it as an attachment, but keep in mind that not everyone can read your attachments. To be able to read a file someone else sends, the other person must have a program that can open that particular type of file.

Sending photographs is pretty easy—digital cameras always create the photographs in the file format called "JPEG," with the three letter extension at the end of ".jpg." Just about anyone should be able to open a JPEG (pronounced *jay peg*).

Exercise 4: Attach a file to an email message.

1 Open a new message, address it, and type your message.

It's *polite* to type a message—don't just send a file without any sort of note! If it's something other than a photograph, it can be helpful to state what kind of file it is and how it was created. ("This is a text file created in Keynote on a Mac using OS X.")

2 Click the "Attach" button in the message window toolbar, or choose "Attach File…" from the File menu. The standard Open dialog box appears so you can find and select the file you wish to attach.

3 Find the file, select it, then click "Open."

If you don't know how to find files in the Open window, please see Chapter 7, *or* skip steps 2 and 3 and use the alternate method explained below.

Alternate method of attaching a file:

Either use the Photo Browser, as shown on the opposite page, or simply drag any file from anywhere on your computer and drop it into a message window.

Exercise 5: Remove an attachment from a message you are sending.

▪ Select the attachment in the "New Message" window (click once on it), then press the Delete key.

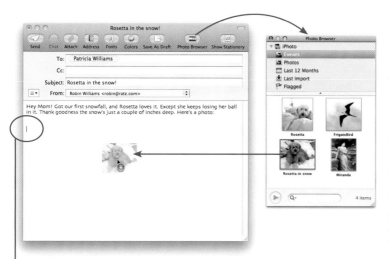

In a "New Message" window, click on the "Photo Browser" icon to see all of your photos that you've stored in iPhoto. Just find the photo you want and drag it into the email message.

The original file does not leave with the email—the original stays right where it is and a **copy** is sent with the email.

Or drag a file from anywhere on your Mac and drop it in the email message window.

The photo will land where the insertion point is flashing (as explained on pages 64–65), so keep your eye on it!

This is what the attachment looks like once I have dropped it into the message area. The recipient can usually just double-click on the icon to open it. Or she can drag it to her Desktop first, and then open it.

Depending on the file, you might see the actual image here in the message pane, and the recipient might also see the actual image. She can still just drag it to her Desktop if she wants to keep it.

Use this menu to make the file a reasonable size for going through the Internet. Less than 200 KB is okay.

Download an attachment that someone sent you

Mail makes it very easy to **download (copy) files from an email** to your Mac. Now, whether you can actually "open" a file someone sent you, once it's on your Desktop, is a completely different matter! If someone sends you a file created in a program you don't have on your Mac, you might not be able to open it. That's not your fault—the person sending the file should ask if you can open that file type, and if not, prepare the file in such a way that you can. But that's a separate big topic.

Keep in mind that you never want to open attachments from someone you don't know!

Exercise 6: Download an attachment someone sent you in an email message.

- Open the email that contains the attachment. Then do *one* of these things:

  Either single-click the "Save" button in the address area (shown below). It will look like nothing happened, but you'll find the file in your Downloads folder (which is in your Home folder, and probably is still in your Dock, next to the Trash can).

  Or drag the file from the email and drop it on your Desktop. You might get a message that says you can't get the file until it has been downloaded; if you do, just tell the message to download the file and you will be able to drag it off.

  Or *press* (instead of *click*) on the "Save" button and choose whether to save individual files into folders or add them directly into iPhoto.

Press on this **Save** button to see your options!

Click the **Quick Look** button to see any attached image up close. If there is more than one image attached, this button says "Slideshow" and will display all the images in a slideshow format. Try it!

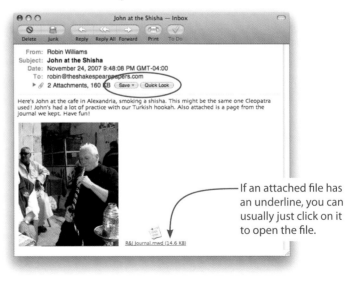

If an attached file has an underline, you can usually just click on it to open the file.

The **Notes** feature in Mail is a handy place to store ideas, thoughts, or any other information you want to keep track of. If you need reminders, though, see the following pages about To Do items!

Create a Note

Exercise: Create a new Note.

1 Click the "Note" button in Mail's toolbar. (This button is only available when you're in the main viewer window, *not when an email message is open and active.* You can create To Do items from email messages, as described on the following pages, but not Notes.)

2 A "New Note" window opens in which you can type a brief or lengthy note. Mail will use your first line of text as the subject of the note (keep that in mind as you write it), and shows the first line in Mail's list of Notes.

Use the toolbar buttons to format your text, add an attachment, or create a To Do item (see next page), just as you would in an email message.

If you "Send" a note, an email window will open with this note inside the message area.

3 If you want an automatically bulleted or numbered list, go to the Format menu at the top of your screen, down to "Lists," and choose the type of list you want. Type your list, hitting a Return after each item. To stop the list so you can type regular text, hit the Return key twice.

4 When finished, click "Done."

As soon as you make your first Note (or To Do item), a new "Reminders" section appears in the Mail sidebar, as shown below. Click "Notes" to display all of them in their own viewer window. You'll also see the Notes appear in your list of email messages when viewing an inbox.

159

Create a To Do List Mail is the message center for your digital life. Use Mail to create To Do lists and Notes so you stay organized and can find all your information quickly and easily. If you use iCal, these To Dos will automatically appear in iCal for you (see the book *Cool Mac Apps* for details on using iCal).

Exercise 1: Create a To Do item *from text in an email message.*

1 Select the text in a message you've received.

2 Click the "To Do" button in Mail's toolbar. You can create as many To Dos from one message as you like.

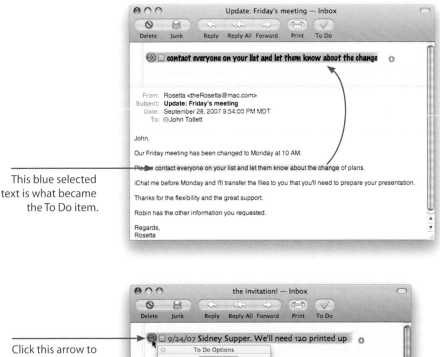

This blue selected text is what became the To Do item.

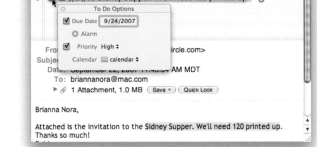

Click this arrow to open the "To Do Options" menu you see here. The due date gets inserted into your To Do text.

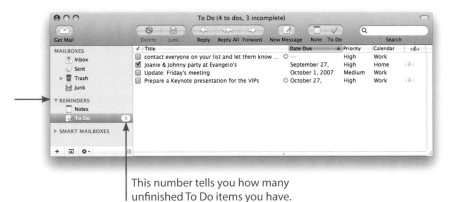

Click the X to delete the item.

Check the box when the To Do is completed.

Click this arrow to show the original email message.

Client meeting — Inbox

Delete   Junk   Reply   Reply All   Forward   Print   To Do

2/5/08 finish the web site estimates
mark your calendar for March 17, 2009
iChat me

From: John Tollett
Subject: **Client meeting**
Date: September 29, 2007 11:16:36 AM MDT
To: Rosetta

Rosetta,

Our big meeting is coming up soon. Did you finish the web site estimates?

Don't forget to mark your calendar for March 17, 2009 and start making plans for hosting the Design Symposium.

Exercise 2: Create a To Do item *related to an email message.*

1. Control-click in a blank area of the message.
2. From the pop-up menu that appears, choose "New To Do." A To Do graphic slides down from the top of the window. Type a brief note.

Exercise 3: Create a To Do item *without an email message.*

1. Click the "To Do" icon in the toolbar.
2. Type your message in the field provided.
3. Control-click on the message to get options for setting priorities, due date, etc.

As soon as you create a To Do item, you'll see a new section in your Mail sidebar called "Reminders." To Dos have their own viewer pane, as shown below, with their own **columns of information.** Control-click on any column header to see what other columns of information you can add.

To Do (4 to dos, 3 incomplete)

Get Mail   Delete   Junk   Reply   Reply All   Forward   New Message   Note   To Do   Search

✓	Title	Date Due	Priority	Calendar	
	contact everyone on your list and let them know ...	--	High	Work	
✓	Joanie & Johnny party at Evangelo's	September 27,	High	Home	
	Update: Friday's meeting	October 1, 2007	Medium	Work	
	Prepare a Keynote presentation for the VIPs	October 27,	High	Work	

MAILBOXES
Inbox
Sent
Trash
Junk

▼ REMINDERS
Notes
To Do   3

▶ SMART MAILBOXES

This number tells you how many unfinished To Do items you have.

161

Address Book

The Address Book icon is in your Dock, your Applications folder, and in the Mail "New Message" toolbar.

The **Address Book** works independently as well as in conjunction with Mail to create Address Cards that store contact information for individuals or groups. When Mail is open, you can automatically create an Address Book entry for anyone who sent mail to you. When you open the Address Book from a new message you're writing, you can automatically address email to an individual or an entire group.

To choose an image, click the Edit button, then double-click this space.
Or drag an image from your Desktop and drop it right in this space.

Once you add an image, it will appear in a chat session with this person and it will appear in any email she sends you.

Search for information on any card; simply enter text.

Switch between this full-column view and a card-only view.

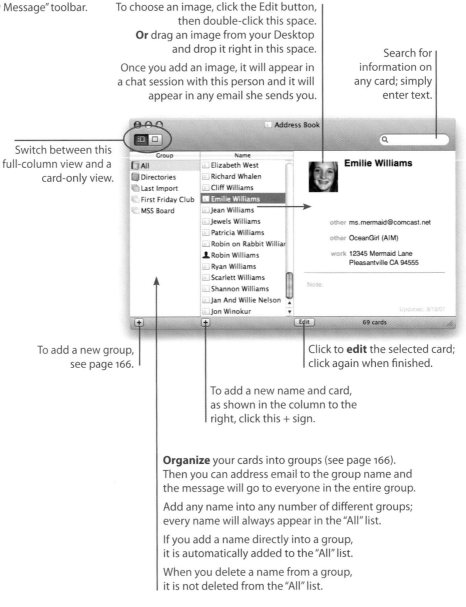

To add a new group, see page 166.

Click to **edit** the selected card; click again when finished.

To add a new name and card, as shown in the column to the right, click this + sign.

Organize your cards into groups (see page 166). Then you can address email to the group name and the message will go to everyone in the entire group.

Add any name into any number of different groups; every name will always appear in the "All" list.

If you add a name directly into a group, it is automatically added to the "All" list.

When you delete a name from a group, it is not deleted from the "All" list.

You can **add a new address card** to the Address Book from either the Address Book or Mail.

Add new names and addresses to Address Book

Exercise 1: Add a new address card while using **Address Book.**

1 Open the Address Book, if it isn't already.

2 Single-click the **+** at the bottom of the "Name" column.

3 This makes a new card automatically appear and the first-name field is already selected for you, waiting for you to type.

4 Type the person's first name, then hit the Tab key, which will automatically select the last-name field.

   Type the last name, then hit Tab, etc. Continue to fill in all the information you know.

5 If a label is changeable, you'll see two tiny arrows. For instance, maybe you want to change the label "mobile" to "cell." Single-click the tiny arrows and you'll get a little pop-up menu, as shown below. Choose one of the pre-named labels, *or* choose "Custom…" and type in the name of the label you want.

6 Click the green **+** sign to add another label and field; click the red **–** sign to delete the label and field to its right. Any field that has no information will not appear on the actual card.

7 When you're finished, click the "Edit" button at the bottom of the card.

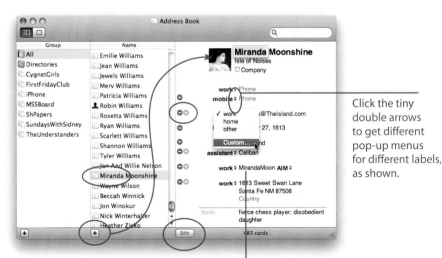

Click the tiny double arrows to get different pop-up menus for different labels, as shown.

If you know this person's AIM name, Buddy name, or Mac.com email address, enter it here so you can use it in **iChat.**

Add a name and address from Mail

You can add anyone's address to your Address Book as soon as they send you an email.

Exercise 2: Add a sender's email address to your Address Book instantly.

1 Make sure you're in the **Mail** program. Either single-click on an email in your list to select it, *or* double-click to open the message.

2 From the "Message" menu in the menu bar across the top of your screen, choose "Add Sender To Address Book," *or* press Command Shift Y. The Address Book will not open, but the sender's address will be added.

Single-click to select a sender's email in your list, then press Command Shift Y.

Check on that address later, though, because if a person's first and last names are not included in their own email address, you'll find the new address in your Address Book at the very top of the "Name" column as <No Name>. **Edit** that card to add the person's name so he is sorted in the list properly.

From your Address Book, you can **send someone an email** easier than returning a self-addressed stamped envelope. This assumes, of course, that you have this person's email address in your Address Book.

Exercise 3: Use your Address Book to send someone an email.

1 Open your Address Book and select the person you want to send email to (single-click his name).

2 Single-click on the tiny label that's to the *left* of the email address. A menu pop ups, as shown below.

Single-click on the label next to the email address to get this pop-up menu.

Tip: Single-click on all the various labels of an address card to get a variety of options, depending on what you click on.

3 Choose "Send Email," and a new message window appears with that person's address in the "To" field.

Exercise 4: Address a message in Mail from the Address Pane.

1 You don't have to go get your Address Book to address a message. In Mail, create a new message, then single-click the "Address" icon in the message toolbar.

2 A limited version of the Address Book opens, as shown below. You can't add or delete addresses at this point, but you can select any number of addresses or groups (Command-click to select more than one), then click the "To" button and those names will go straight to the email.

Address an email
message in Mail
using the
Address Pane

This is the Address Pane, a limited version of your Address Book.

Make a group mailing list

If you regularly send email to a specific group of people, you can make a **group list in your Address Book** so with one click of the button your email will be sent to everyone on the list.

PLEASE don't stick everyone in your whole dang Address Book in a group list!!! Not everyone wants you to forward every joke and every virus warning (which Macs don't get anyway)!

Create groups that have specific purposes. You might want one group list just for family members, another for your poker club, one you send your travelogues to, and one for those people who have called you up and said, "Please put me on your mailing list for every stupid joke that runs across the Internet!" Have a separate list for people who really want political ads, too.

Anyway, it's easy to make a group list, and it's easy to send a message to one or more groups at once.

To make a group list:

1. First go ahead and put everyone you want in your Address Book. Their names have to be in your Address Book before you can put them in a list.

2. Single-click the plus sign (**+**) at the bottom of the "Group" pane.

3. In the field for the new group that appears, type the name of your group.

4. Single-click the "All" list.

5. Drag names from the All list in the "Name" pane and drop them into the new group.

   You can put the same name in any number of groups; all names will always be in the All list.

To send email to a group list:

- Simply type the name of the group in the "To" field.

Send email to a
group mailing list

**To make sure the recipients do not see the entire list
of email addresses:**

1   In **Mail,** go to the Mail preferences (in the Mail menu).

2   Click the "Composing" icon in the toolbar.

3   Make sure there is **no** checkmark in the option "When
sending to a group, show all member addresses."

  This is the polite thing to do. All of us get too much
  mail and it's not a good idea to give everyone on your
  list the actual addresses of everyone else.

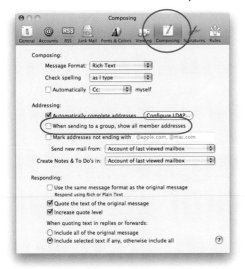

Have your mail read out loud to you:

1   Open an email message.

2   Press-and-drag over the text that you want to read out
loud, *or* hit Command A to select all.

3   Control-click anywhere in the selected message.
From the contextual menu that pops up, slide down
to "Speech," then out to "Start Speaking."

  You can go work on anything else you like on your Mac
  and your mail will be read to you.

  The speech feature uses the voice you last chose in
  the System Preferences for Speech. (Click the System
  Preferences icon in the Dock, click the "Speech" icon,
  then click the "Text to Speech" tab, and choose a voice.)

4   To stop the voice, repeat step 3 and choose "Stop Speaking."

Have your mail read
out loud to you

This is
the System
Preferences icon.

Remember

- Do not type an email in **ALL CAPS.** Since we can't hear voices in an email, all caps is the visual equivalent of shouting. And it's just as annoying in print as it is in person.

- It's very easy to make a group mailing list. But don't send email to a list of people unless you *know* everyone on that list *wants* to receive that mail. **Ask first** before putting someone on your list, please!

- When you **forward a message** to someone, please take a few seconds to get rid of all the superfluous garbage that ends up in a forwarded message. The easy way to do this is to select just the actual lines you want to forward *before* you click the Forward button.

- You can have your **email read out loud** to you with the click of a button! See page 167.

Other Useful Features 12

Well, if you've worked through all of the exercises in this "little" book, you should be pretty comfortable with your Mac by now. This chapter introduces you to a couple of other features that you will need to know as you spend more time with your computer.

Good luck! *Now forward—in all directions!*

System Preferences

The System Preferences allow you to change the settings of a number of features on your computer. This will become a familiar process to you as you work with your Mac. In this little book, all I can do is point you to the System Preferences and suggest you check them out. Most of them are very self-explanatory.

This is the System Preferences icon that is probably in your Dock.

To open System Preferences:

- The icon shown to the left should be in your Dock. Single-click on it.

- Or you can always go to the Apple menu and choose "System Preferences... ."

Tip: If you want everything on your screen to appear larger, click the **"Displays"** icon and choose a **lower numbered** resolution.

To open a preference pane, single-click any icon. The new pane will **replace** the one you see.

To come back to this main pane, single-click the "Show All" button in the upper-left of the window, or press Command L.

This is an example of the kind of thing System Preferences can do for you: The **Desktop & Screen Saver** preferences pane lets you customize the appearance of your Desktop and provides some amazing options for screen savers (which are animated graphics that appear on your screen when you're not using your Mac).

In System Preferences, click the **Desktop** tab (circled below) to display the Desktop preferences. You can choose the background of your Desktop. Change the color or choose a photograph or one of the abstract images provided in the folders shown below. You can also use any photo or graphic image that's in your Pictures folder: choose "Pictures Folder" from the scrolling list pane shown below.

Or choose "iPhoto Albums" and choose any photo or graphic image you have stored in iPhoto.

When you select a folder in the list, its contents are shown in the pane on the right. Select an image and it immediately appears in the thumbnail image space, and also on the Desktop.

Desktop & Screen Saver

Desktop & Screen Saver

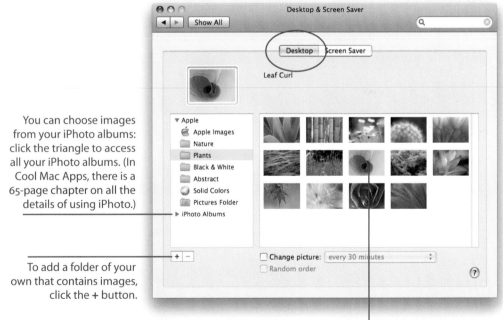

You can choose images from your iPhoto albums: click the triangle to access all your iPhoto albums. (In Cool Mac Apps, there is a 65-page chapter on all the details of using iPhoto.)

To add a folder of your own that contains images, click the + button.

Single-click any image to turn it into the background on your monitor.

Aliases

Methinks I scent the morning air

An alias looks just like the original icon, but there's a small arrow in the bottom-left corner.

An **alias** is an "empty" icon that represents the real thing. You create aliases so you don't have to go find the original file every-time you want to use it—you can put aliases where they are easier to find, and keep the originals in their important folders.

You can make aliases of applications, documents, folders, utili-ties, games, etc. Aliases are wonderful tools for organizing your work— anything you want to use is only one double-click away from wherever you are. Remember, an alias is just a picture that goes and gets the real file.

Exercise: Making an alias is so easy.

1 Select the item you want to make an alias of (click once on it).

Make an alias

2 Then choose one of these four ways to make an alias:

Either from the File menu, choose "Make Alias."

Or press Command L.

Or hold down the Control key and single-click on the item you want to make an alias of. A contextual menu pops up, as shown below; choose "Make Alias."

After you choose "Make Alias," the new alias will be sitting right on top of the original file. Just drag it to where you want to keep it.

Or hold down Command Option and drag the file— if you drag it to a different folder or to the Desk-top, when you let go you'll have an alias with the word "alias" removed from its name; if you drag to somewhere else in the same folder, you'll have an alias with the word "alias" at the end of it.

Drag the alias icon to wherever you want to keep it. Rename it if you like. The new file does not have to have the word "alias" in its name. And it doesn't matter if you move the original file—the alias can always find it.

Making aliases is easy, but here are some **details** you should understand.

- An alias isn't a *duplicate* of anything; it's just a **pointer** to the real thing. If you double-click an *alias* of Quicken, for instance, it will open your *original* Quicken application, even if the original Quicken is stored in a completely different folder.

- If you **delete** an alias, you don't delete the original—the original is still stored on your hard disk. So you can keep revising your filing system as your needs change. Don't want that alias of Budget Charts cluttering up your Project Plans folder any more? Fine; throw it away. The original Budget Charts is still where you stored it.

- If you put an item into an *alias* of a **folder,** the item actually gets put into the *original* folder.

- You can **move** an alias and even **rename** an alias. The Mac will still be able to find the original and open it whenever you double-click on the alias.

- Even if you move or rename the **original** file, the alias can still find it.

- If you **delete** the *original* file, the Mac does *not* automatically delete any of the aliases you created for that file. When you double-click on an alias whose original has been trashed, you will get a message telling you the original could not be located.

Details of aliases

Note: Items in the Dock, the Sidebar, or a Finder window Toolbar are already aliases.

Search for Files on your Mac with Spotlight

No matter how well organized you keep your Mac, one day it's going to be difficult to **find a particular file.** Perhaps you misplaced it or you copied it from somewhere and can't find it or you don't even know where it went in the first place. **Spotlight** can find anything and everything for you. It finds the text you're looking for whether it's in the name of the file, inside an email message, a pdf, or in the text of a document.

Tips for searching: It doesn't matter whether you type capital or lower case letters—the search will find "Love Letter" even if you search for "love letter."

Spaces, however, do matter. That is, "love letter" will not find "loveletter."

If you don't know the exact name of the file, just type any part of it that you think is in the file name, such as "love."

Exercise: Do a quick and easy search.

1 Open any Finder window.

2 Type part of the name of the file you're looking for into the search field. As soon as you start typing, the search begins and items appear in a list in the Finder window, as shown on the opposite page.

As you continue typing, the search narrows to match the word or phrase you've typed, and the list of found items changes as you type.

This is the search field.

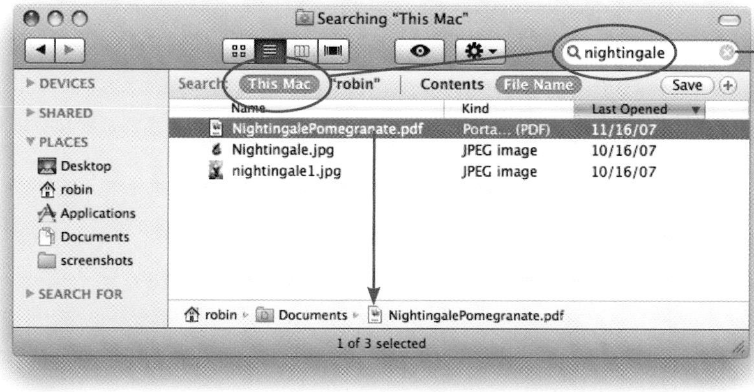

To get your normal window back, click the **X**. This deletes everything from the search field.

3 Another thing happens as you begin to type: A search bar appears with locations in which to search. In the example above, you can see it is currently searching "This Mac." Click any other option you see in that tab to search that specific area.

To search only in a specific folder, first select that folder *before* you begin the search process.

4 Select one of the *found* items in the list, and the bottom section of the Finder window displays the *location* of that selected file, as shown above.

To open the selected file, double-click it.

To open the window in which the selected file is stored, press Command R.

5 **To get information** about that particular file, single-click a file and press Command I to get the Info window, as shown to the right.

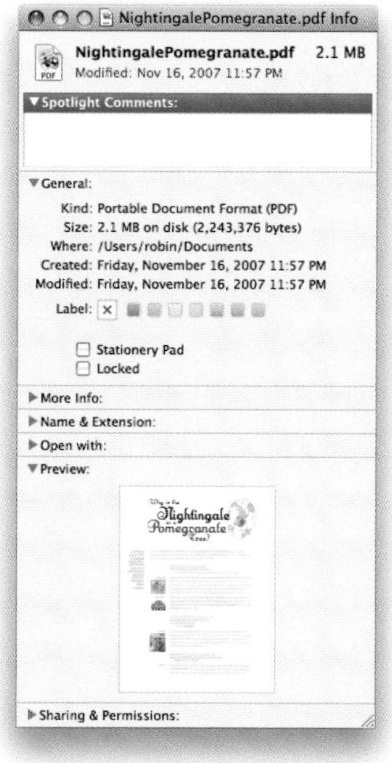

—continued

175

Narrow the search   You can get even more specific with a search. Follow the steps on the previous pages. Plus:

- Click the **+** button to add a parameter. Each time you click a **+** button, you'll add another parameter.

  Of course, click a **–** button to delete a parameter.

- Each parameter can be changed: single click on it and choose something else, if you like.

  Each parameter has specific options you can change: single-click on the menu to its right and choose the options. You'll see different options for each parameter. Some will display fields in which you can enter information. The best way to learn how to use it is to experiment!

Find types of files   Leave the search field blank and use just the parameters (as explained above) to find files. For instance, you can find every "Image" you have opened "Since Yesterday" or as shown below, I found every "Presentation" I have stored on this Mac.

If you *do* add a search term in the field, you can limit the search even further—you might want to find every "Image" you opened "Since Yesterday" that has the word "heart" involved.

In this example, the search field is blank. I set the parameters to find every presentation, regardless of its name.

The search in every application on the Mac is powered by Spotlight. For instance, take another look at the Viewer window in **Mail** (page 150)—that search field in the upper-right corner is powered by Spotlight.

In **Address Book,** select a person's card. Then hold down the Command key and click on the name; you'll get a contextual menu in which you can choose to Spotlight that person, as shown below. Every email to or from that person or in which that person is mentioned will be found, plus every relevant file on your Mac.

Spotlight in applications

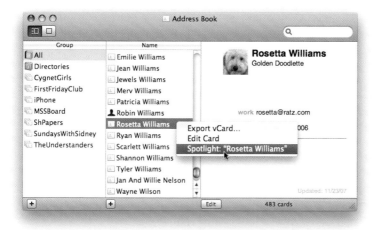

In **Safari, TextEdit, Preview** or in any **Mail** message, Control-click to get a menu that includes an option to "Search in Spotlight."

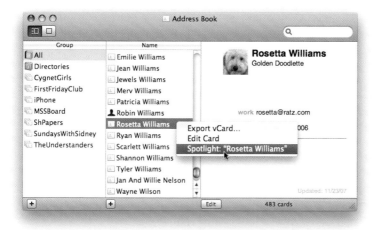

Experiment in other applications!

Stickies

Stickies

The **Stickies** application lets you put little Stickie notes all over your screen, just like you'd stick them around the edge of your monitor (my kids tell me my monitor looks like a giant daisy). **The Stickies application is inside your Applications folder.**

Grocery list

* yogurt
* avocados
* brown rice
* green drink
* chicken
* red wine

Brianna Nora's birthday is coming up soon! Don't forget!

Board of Directors Meeting Mary Sidney Society

Created: Monday, September 24, 2007
9:54:33 PM MT
Modified: Monday, September 24, 2007
9:54:33 PM MT

Notice in the examples above you can see these features:

- **Change fonts, size, color,** etc., just as in any other Mac application, using the Font dialog box (press Command T).

- Double-click in the title bar of any Stickie note to "roll it up" so **just the title bar shows,** as you can see above ("Board of Directors Meeting"). The first line of type appears in the title bar. Double-click the title bar again to unroll the note.

- Mouse over any note to display a **tool tip** that gives you information about the note, as shown above.

- Drag a **graphic** image from anywhere on your Mac and drop it into the Stickie note.

- A note can hold many pages of text and graphics. You won't see **scroll** bars, but you can drag the mouse through the text and it will scroll, or use the arrow keys or the PageUp or PageDown keys. Resize a Stickie note just as you would any other window—drag the bottom-right corner.

- Notice the red dots under the name "Brianna." This is a visual clue that the **spell checker** is on and working.

- If you prefer working with a certain font and a certain size and a certain color note, you can **set a default** so all your notes look like that without having to select your favorite specifications for every note. Just set up one note the way you like it, then go to the Note menu and choose "Use as Default." All new notes will have those specifications.

- The grocery note you see on the opposite page is a **bulleted list.**

   To make such a list, Command Option-click on the note and choose "List…" from the contextual menu that appears. You can choose from a variety of bullets and numbers, plus you can add a prefix and suffix to the bullet. Thus you could create a numbered list that uses **(1)** or **Act 1:** or •A• or any other combination. The list options even include Greek charac-ters and Asian characters.

   To start the list, hit Option Tab before you type the first item in the list.

   To continue the list, just hit a Return after each item. You can hit Option Tab Tab to indent an extra level.

   To end the list, hit Return twice.

   You can **change the bullet formatting** at any time— just use the List options from the contextual menu as explained above.

In the File menu there are two **print** options:

- The option to "Print Active Note" prints the Stickie that's in front of all the others, which is called the "active" note. Be careful! If a Stickie note is rolled up so only its title bar is visible, it still might be the active note. To make sure, first click on the note you want to print.

- The option to "Print All Notes" prints all of your Stickie notes one after another. Each one is not on a separate piece of paper—they are all run together.

The Thunder's Mouth

O that my tongue were in the thunder's mouth!
Then with a passion would I shake the world.

Said Constance in King John

Burn a CD or DVD with a Burn Folder

This section explains how to burn **data** CDs and DVDs.

If you want to burn **music CDs,** use iTunes: First create a Playlist in iTunes, then insert a blank CD-R, and burn the Playlist to the CD-R.

You'll want to create backups of your important work so you'll be sure to have it in case anything happens to your computer. The easiest way to make a backup is to **burn a CD or DVD.**

The steps below describe how to burn "data files" (as opposed to music or movies) onto a disc.

The **Burn Folder** is the easiest way to burn a CD or DVD. You'll drag items into this special folder, and when you're ready, burn the contents to a disc. Your Mac automatically creates **aliases** of those files (see pages 172–173 for details on aliases). This means that after you burn the disc, you can throw away the entire Burn Folder without destroying any original files.

The wonderful thing is that you can collect items you want to burn without having to actually burn the disc at that moment—you can collect files over the period of a project and when finished, you have a folder ready to back up onto a disc.

Exercise: Create a Burn Folder, put files inside, and burn it.

1 Open a Finder window. Select the window in which you want the Burn Folder to appear. For instance, single-click on your Home icon in the Sidebar, *or* single-click the Documents folder icon. *Or* click on the Desktop, if you want the folder to appear there. (You can always move the Burn Folder to wherever you like, of course.)

2 From the File menu, choose "New Burn Folder."

3 A folder with the "Burn" icon on it appears in the selected window.

Burn Folder

4 **To put a file in the folder** so you can burn it later, just drag the original file and drop it into the Burn Folder. Your Mac will put an *alias* of the file into the Burn Folder and the original will stay right where it was, safe and sound.

5 **To burn the folder onto a s,** first insert a blank CD-R or DVD (hold down the Eject key to open or close the disc drawer, if you have one—the Eject key is in the upper-right corner of your keyboard, with a triangle/ bar symbol on it).

You will be asked to name the disc, which of course you should do.

6 **Then** double-click the Burn Folder; a bar across the top of the window appears with a "Burn" button, as shown below. Click the "Burn" button in the window.

I put the Burn Folder in my Home folder. Then I dragged it into my Sidebar, as you can see above, so it's always easily available.

If you drag the Burn Folder into the Sidebar, as shown above, it displays a "burn" icon next to its name. After you've put all the files you want to save into the Burn Folder, you can just single-click that burn icon to start the process.

This is the burn icon.

You can make as many Burn Folders as you want. Rename them as you do any other folder. This makes it easy to have a separate Burn Folder for each project.

If you change your mind and want to take an unburned disc out of the Mac, Control-click (or right-click) on the disc icon and choose "Eject '_____ CD.'"

Exposé

Exposé is a feature built into your Mac that lets you **manage the open windows** on your Desktop. For instance, you might have TextEdit open with a word processing document on your screen, plus your Safari browser for surfing the web, plus Mail so you can keep up with your email, and maybe the System Preferences because you're setting up some new customization. That can create quite a mess, and that's what Exposé takes care of. Experi-ment with the following keyboard shortcuts.

- **Hide every window so you can see your entire Desktop:** Press F11 (that's an Fkey at the top of your keyboard, not the letter F and the number 11!). Everything will disappear, but don't freak out! Just press F11 to bring all the windows back again.

- **Show just application windows** (no Finder windows): Press F10.

- **Show every window on the screen at once,** as shown below-right: Press F9.

  While in this view, mouse over a window and a little message pops up telling you what that is. Single-click on any window to bring just that window to the front— all the others will stay hidden.

And here's **another tip for keeping your Desktop uncluttered.** Whenever you move from one application to another, hold down the **Option key** before you click on another icon in the Dock or on the Desktop. The Option key hides the application you are currently in. Try it!

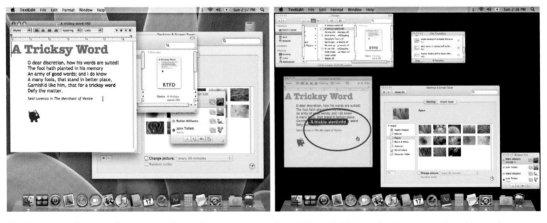

This is a typical messy Desktop with windows all over the place.

Press F9 and all the windows organize themselves so you can see each one. Single-click on the one you want to be in front.

Dashboard provides quick access to information customized just for you, by you, displayed in the form of **widgets.** The widgets pop up in front of you with the click of a key and disappear just as quickly with another click of a key. You can see what time it is in cities around the world, check the weather in the town where your mother lives, access a dictionary and thesaurus, track the flights of planes, use a calculator, and much more.

Below you see an example of Dashboard with selected widgets showing, plus the **Widgets Bar** along the bottom. The widgets appear on top of whatever's on your screen so you don't have to move anything out of the way.

To make Dashboard appear or disappear, tap the F12 key (it's above the Delete key on your keyboard). Or click the Dashboard icon in the Dock (shown to the right).

To make the Widget Bar appear or disappear, single-click the + sign in the bottom-left corner of your screen. As you can see below, once you show the Widget Bar, the + sign becomes an **X**; click the **X** to hide the Widget Bar.

Dashboard: Widgets at your fingertips

This is the Dashboard icon.

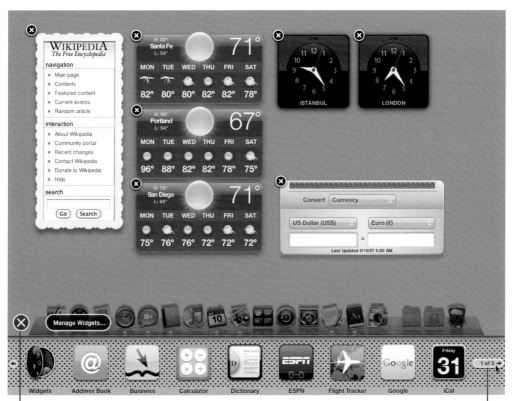

To hide or show this Widgets Bar, click this button.

As you can see, your screen darkens when you display Dashboard, and the widgets appear on top.

To see more widgets in this bar, click this button.

Add or delete widgets from your Dashboard

To add widgets to your Dashboard or **to remove them,** first display the Widgets Bar, as explained on the previous page.

- **To add a widget,** single-click its icon in the Widget Bar. The widget will appear in the Dashboard. Drag it into the position you want.

- **To remove a widget,** click the **x** in its upper-left corner. If you don't see the **x**, hold down the Option key to show it, then click it to remove the widget.

Click this to remove the widget from your Dashboard.

Work with widgets

I'll show you how to work with a few of the widgets, and you'll quickly see how easy it is to work with all of them.

Many widgets display a tiny letter "*i*" when your pointer gets near a corner (it's not always in the same corner on each widget). When you see that little "*i*," single-click on it to flip the widget over. If you can flip it over, you'll often find preferences for that particular widget, as shown below. Click "Done" to flip it back to the front side.

Flip over the weather widget to change the preferences.

Type in a city and state (or country), then hit Enter.

Use the **Translation** widget to translate from one language to another. Click the snake-like button to reverse the languages.

It's very interesting to translate a phrase or sentence into another language, then translate it back into English.

Convert just about any sort of measurement from one unit to another with the **Unit Converter.** The "Currency" option goes to the Internet to get the current exchange rate. Use the menus on both sides of the Unit Converter (left and right sides) to choose what's being converted to what.

From the Convert menu, choose the sort of conversion you want.

From the left and right sides, choose the specific items you want to have converted.

The **Dictionary** widget looks up words for you, as shown below. Choose "Thesaurus" from its menu to find synonyms.

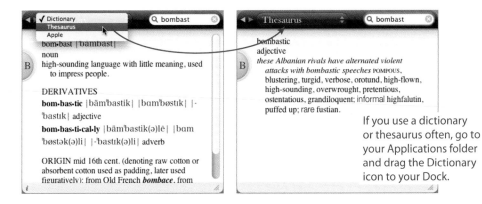

If you use a dictionary or thesaurus often, go to your Applications folder and drag the Dictionary icon to your Dock.

To change the picture in the Tile Game puzzle:

1 When Dashboard is open, click the **+** to display the Widgets Bar.

2 Put the "Tile Game" on your screen.

3 Close Dashboard.

4 In the Finder, find the picture you want to use in the tile puzzle. Start dragging it to nowhere in particular.

5 While you are dragging (don't let go of the mouse), press F12 to open Dashboard.

6 Drop the picture you're dragging onto the tile puzzle.

This is the original puzzle.

Now the puzzle is my dog, Rosetta.

185

Display more than one widget

You can display multiple copies of any kind of widget. For instance, you might like to view the flight paths of a number of different flights, open several dictionary widgets to compare words, or view the weather for each of the cities where your children live.

Just click on a widget more than once to put more than one in the Dashboard. Each one lands directly on top of the one before, so you'll have to drag them off of each other!

Manage your widgets

You can get rid of widgets that you never use so they don't take up space in your Widgets Bar, and you can get more widgets from Apple's site to add to your collection. Use the Widgets Manager.

Exercise: Use the Widgets Manager to delete or add widgets.

1 When Dashboard is open, click the **+** to display the Widgets Bar.

2 In the Widgets Bar, single-click on either the "Manage Widgets…" button *or* on the "Widgets" icon, as shown to the left.

You'll get the Widgets Manager, as shown below.

3 **To remove a widget,** uncheck its checkbox.

To find and add widgets, click the "More Widgets…" button. This takes you to Apple's web site where you'll find hundreds of terrific widgets, almost all of which are free. Choose one to download, and your Mac will copy it to your computer and install it for you.

186

In the Apple menu the last four options are **Sleep, Restart, Shut Down,** and **Log Out.** Here is a brief description of when you might use each of these options.

- **Sleep** does two things: 1) It turns off the monitor display so your screen goes black, which is especially good for flat panels, and 2) it stops the hard disk from spinning. Both of these features save energy. If your machine goes to sleep, tap any of the keys on your keyboard to make it wake up again.

- **Restart** shuts down your Mac and starts it up again without ever turning off the power. This is easier on the computer than turning off the power and rebooting (turning it back on). You often have to restart after installing new software (or anytime things just start acting weird).

- On **Shut Down,** the Mac takes care of internal business, cleans up everything, and turns itself off (it actually turns off the power).

  Shut Down when you are done for the day or longer. Actually, you rarely have to Shut Down in Mac OS X—you can leave your machine on for weeks at a time, setting it to sleep automatically after a certain number of idle minutes. Since installing OS X, I leave my computer on for days on end.

- Use **Log Out** to switch between multiple users. If you are the only user, you can use it as a safety precaution when you are going to be away from your computer for a while. Log Out brings up a "Log in" screen where you must type your administrator password to get back to your Desktop. (The administrator password is the one that you set up the first time you turned on your Mac. Don't lose that password!!)

Sleep, Restart, Shut Down, or Log Out

I can't cover multiple users in this small book; use the Accounts pane in the System Preferences, and if you need help, please see the more advanced book, *Mac OS X 10.5 Leopard: Peachpit Learning Series.*

- Make an **alias** if you find that you are constantly digging into a particular folder to find a particular file. Or make an alias of the entire folder and put the folder alias right on your Desktop.

- Use the **System Preferences** to customize just about everything on your Mac.

- You can **burn** data files (text, photographs, etc.) to a CD using the method described in this chapter, but to burn music CDs that you can listen to in any player, use iTunes to create a playlist and burn the CD. (Detailed directions for using iTunes are in the *Cool Mac Apps* book because they wouldn't fit in this book!)

Index

Colophon

I wrote, designed, and did the layout, production, and index of this book in Adobe InDesign on my Mac Pro. The body copy font is Warnock Pro, the sans serif is Myriad Pro, both from Adobe. The chapter heads are LaPortenia from the Umbrella foundry, available at Veer.com.

Accent marks

See page 79 if you're not sure how to type accent marks.

Tilde	Press	Let go, then press
~	Option n	Spacebar
ã	Option n	a
Ã	Option n	Shift a
ñ	Option n	n
Ñ	Option n	Shift n
õ	Option n	o
Õ	Option n	Shift o

Diaeresis	Press	Let go, then press
··	Option u	Spacebar
ä	Option u	a
Ä	Option u	Shift a
ë	Option u	e
Ë	Option u	Shift e
ï	Option u	i
Ï	Option Shift f	
ö	Option u	o
Ö	Option u	Shift o
ü	Option u	u
Ü	Option u	Shift u
ÿ	Option u	y

Circumflex	Press	Let go, then press
^	Option i	Spacebar
â	Option i	a
Â	Option Shift m	
ê	Option i	e
Ê	Option i	Shift e
î	Option i	i
Î	Option Shift d	
ô	Option i	o
Ô	Option Shift j	
û	Option i	u
Û	Option i	Shift u

Acute	Press	Let go, then press
´	Option e	Spacebar
á	Option e	a
Á	Option e *or* Option Shift y	Shift a
é	Option e	e
É	Option e	Shift e
í	Option e	i
Í	Option e *or* Option Shift s	Shift i
ó	Option e	o
Ó	Option e *or* Option Shift h	Shift o
ú	Option e	u
Ú	Option e *or* Option Shift ;	Shift u

Grave	Press	Let go, then press
`	Option ` (` is next to 1, or next to Spacebar; the same key as the regular ~ key)	Spacebar
à	Option `	a
À	Option `	Shift a
è	Option `	e
È	Option `	Shift e
ì	Option `	i
Ì	Option `	Shift i
ò	Option `	o
Ò	Option ` *or* Option Shift l (letter el)	Shift o
ù	Option `	u
Ù	Option `	Shift u

Miscellaneous	Press
å	Option a
Å	Option Shift a
ç	Option c
Ç	Option Shift c

Special characters

The following is a list of the most often-used **special characters.** Remember, hold down the "modifier keys," the ones that don't do anything by themselves, then tap the character key just once.

"	Option [	opening double quote
"	Option Shift [	closing double quote
'	Option]	opening single quote
'	Option Shift]	closing single quote; apostrophe
–	Option Hyphen	en dash
—	Option Shift Hyphen	em dash
…	Option ;	ellipsis *(this character can't be separated at the end of a line as three periods can)*
•	Option 8	bullet *(easy to remember because it's the asterisk key)*
fi	Option Shift 5	ligature of f and i
fl	Option Shift 6	ligature of f and l
©	Option g	
™	Option 2	
®	Option r	
°	Option Shift 8	degree symbol (e.g., 102°F)
¢	Option $	
€	Option Shift 2	Euro symbol
/	Option Shift 1 (one)	fraction bar *(this doesn't descend below the line like the slash does)*
¡	Option 1 (one)	
¿	Option Shift ?	
£	Option 3	
ç	Option c	
Ç	Option Shift c	

Remember, to set an **accent mark** over a letter, press the Option key and the letter (it will look like nothing happened), then press the letter you want under it (see page 79). A complete chart is on the previous two pages.

´	Option e
`	Option ~ (upper-left or next to the Spacebar)
¨	Option u
~	Option n
^	Option i